HEAD, HEART, AND HABIT

BUILDING A LIFE YOU LOVE

PRIYANKA SHIRAVADEKAR

INDIA • SINGAPORE • MALAYSIA

ISBN

Paperback 979-8-89632-962-6
Hardcase 979-8-89699-789-4

To My Dearest Dad

(Shri Ram Mehndiratta ji)

I miss you every single day. Thank you for raising us to be grateful, kind, and loving. I feel so blessed to be your daughter, with parents as compassionate and generous as you and Mom. Whenever I feel lost, I remind myself of the wisdom you would have shared. Thank you for being my best friend and for always standing by me when I needed you.

You taught me to believe, to love, and to be free.
I can be whatever I wish to be, I am with thee.
A lifelong and many lifetimes later,
A promise to be by my side forever.
While a different world waited for your kindness,
You had to tend to the call for this lifetime to end.
While I walk here in the wilderness, missing a friend,
finding my way through the meandering bends.
Until I found you with me etched in my writings,
A reminder of what 'love' means, a little nudge to remind,
I can be whatever I wish to be.

– Love,
Priyanka

Contents

Acknowledgements *7*
Preface *9*

1. Who are You? 13
2. A Way to Express Yourself 20
3. Listen to Your Inner Voice 31
4. Acknowledge Your Fears 36
5. Who is Your Mirror? 45
6. Identify the Weeds Around You 52
7. Imperfection is Perfect 59
8. Mistake? Learn and Retake! 66
9. Love Yourself: You Are Your First Customer 74
10. Believe in Gratitude 83
11. Never Forget Kindness 87
12. Fuel a Passion 91
13. Every Day is an Opportunity to Learn 95
14. Challenge Yourself 99
15. One Step at a Time 102
16. Record Your Successes 106
17. Financial Literacy Starts Early 109

18. Share Responsibility, Build Lasting Trust 117

19. One Mouth, Two Ears: Words Are Power 125

20. Less Clutter, More Focus 135

21. Drive Your Own Car and Take Control 145

22. Heal to Reveal, Meditate to Elevate 153

23. Keep Smiling and Let It Shine 158

24. Look Back and Learn: Embracing Failures 162

25. Simple Actions: One Day or Day One 167

Author Bio *173*

Acknowledgements

I am truly grateful to my family for inspiring me to embark on this writing journey. A special thank you to my dearest daughter, Tanishka, whose presence as my muse ignited countless ideas and encouraged me to share my story. Without the unwavering support and love of my husband, Pritam, I wouldn't have had the space to pause and reflect on my own life's path. Ferro, you are behind me wherever I go, assuring me of the endless love you possess for me. I am deeply thankful to my Mom and Dad, Aai Pappa, sisters, nieces, colleagues and friends for their belief in my potential. The anecdotes I'm about to share would not have been possible without all the wonderful people I've met all along the way. I also extend my heartfelt gratitude to Mirra for her insightful guidance, which helped shape and deepen my reflections.

Preface

We are all on a journey, each carrying our own burdens, whether heavy or light. You don't need to be in a train, airplane, or any mode of transport to be called a traveller. Our journey begins the moment we are born into this world. As we live each day, we unknowingly accumulate a wealth of experiences. This treasure trove of wisdom is sometimes locked away, and we forget where the key is hidden. There are moments in life when we could tap into this reservoir to guide us through difficult times. Unfortunately, we are often unaware that this invaluable wisdom exists, lost somewhere in the depths of the unknown.

I'm Priyanka, a fellow traveller who has learned the art of recognising and reflecting on life's experiences, preparing myself for the journey that still lies ahead. My story begins with an interesting start—I was the youngest of four daughters in my family. All credit for who I am today goes to my family who helped shape me into someone resilient, competitive, and determined.

As a young, free-spirited soul, I was eager to chase my dreams and never took "no" for an answer. I owe a lot to my dad, who was always by my side, ensuring I stayed on the right path. My mom, too, played a pivotal role in reminding me of spreading my wings. Every morning, she would wake me up with inspiring stories of great leaders, reminding me of the boundless potential within all of us. To this day when I have a family of my own, she remains my inspiration, especially when I reflect on how she single-handedly managed the household, four spirited (mostly rebellious) daughters, and her full-time job as a schoolteacher.

In the early 2000s, when India was just beginning to embrace the idea of sending children to different cities for education, I moved away and lived on my own. I was fortunate to have the support of my family, becoming the first one amongst us to be brave and venture out independently.

The trust endowed by my dad gave me a reason to dream more and discover who I am. A new life in a new city after marriage and thereafter another journey to follow my dreams wouldn't have been possible without the support from my husband Pritam, dearest darling daughter Tanishka and my in-laws. In these almost four decades, I filled the treasure chests with my exposure, experience and education as I continued to aspire for more. Furthermore, I didn't lock these treasure chests and kept tapping into them every single day to learn from them. The past teaches us how to improve our present and the present allows us to dream for a better future. With every step we leave the past, present becomes past, and we step into the future.

My plan was to step forwards but with knowledge I received from the previous steps. My objective of sharing my experiences with you is to spark your memories to remind you of how valuable your experience is. Herein, I have shared my journey in the world of IT, how I traversed difficult choices, moved continents and built a network of trusted allies, who have contributed to my success and still do. This book is a gentle nudge, how we can take anything easily available for granted at one point and realise later that it is no more accessible. The busy lives we live can distract us from living a conscious life wherein we understand who we are under layers of wraps that exist, hiding our true self.

I wish to introduce you to your true self by sharing my story, exercises that worked for me in my search for me. The stories I share aren't exceptional but real stories that we all may experience in our walks of life. I hope you enjoy reading the book and invest time in understanding how life can be more meaningful when you know what you are cut out for. With that, I would like to wish you success in whatever you do in this journey called- 'Life'! Happy reading!

Section 1
Understanding Self

For the most part of my life, I remained un-introduced to myself. In fact, I never realised the importance of it. In this section, I have collected the experiences that taught me the importance of self-discovery, tuning to my inner-voice and developing self-belief. Simple life-experiences taught me to harness the value of mentors to continuously evolve as a person. All these collectively built a 'confident' me who was ready for the curve balls thrown. I learnt to accept my weaknesses and leverage my strengths more in whatever I did. I stopped looking for a perfect rainbow or a perfect person, my pleasures are in existence. Being in the present moment completely aided my desire to achieve happiness.

"Your vision will become clear only when you can look into your own heart. Who looks outside, dreams; who looks inside, awakes."

– Carl Jung

Chapter 1
Who are You?

After a perfect day at school, I arrived home with my hunger pangs taking over my intellect and the only thought that clouded my mind was relishing a warm meal.

"Mom, I am hungry!" I yelled as I headed into our house with my aggravated sniffing sense to establish what's there for lunch.

"Oh, you are home! Wash your hands and change. It is your favourite kidney beans and rice". Mom replied to my bellows calmly.

"Don't stay up watching Television all afternoon, take a nap. We are going to a wedding this evening." She added as I gobbled the food with my eyeballs stuck on Michael Jackson's incredible dance moves in a music video on one of the most popular music channels. Tuning to the Music channel while mom prepared a hot meal was a ritual that I relished.

"I have ironed your dress and paired it with the golden sandals; make sure you find a clean pair of frilled white socks in your wardrobe upstairs". Mom ordered authoritatively to get my attention for a minute.

It was time for her afternoon nap, and she reminded me of these worldly duties to switch off the TV and finish my homework. I continued watching the music videos, flipping between MTV and Channel V while I started finishing my science homework until I heard the doorbell ring.

"Who is it? I screamed from the living room without trying to get up from the couch.

When the doorbell rang again and I couldn't hear any response, I rushed to the door with all my might.

"Open the door Pichu, what are you up to!" Dad exclaimed from the other side.

I opened the door and gave a big welcome hug to my dad, excited to see him home earlier than usual and apologised for the delay in getting to the door.

"How was your day at school? Did you do anything interesting?" He smiled and kissed me on the cheek as he asked about my day at school to strike a conversation.

"The day was ok; I sat next to Ritu. She is super talkative and got me into trouble with Mrs. Fernandes at one point. The science lesson was the most exciting part of the day. I am learning about DNA and how it influences our looks, characteristics etc. DNA is our unique identity. I have shown so much interest in the topic that my science teacher has asked me to take part in a declamation on Genetics- role of DNA next month" I blasted out in a breath.

"Sounds interesting. You must tell me more about it. Identity is important. DNA is within you and creates your physical appearance, making you unique. That's how I can recognise that you are my daughter, and you look like me; you've got our family nose. Imagine if we all looked alike? However, there are other traits that are not physical but will build your personal identity. You will learn who you are. So yes, the DNA but also remember PNA". Dad smiled as he explained to me.

"PNA?" I had a big question mark on my face.

"Priyanka's Natural Attributes" He busted into laughter and left me thinking what a discovery!

Our conversation went on with my unlimited questions until we were interrupted by mum walking into the room reminding us to get ready for the wedding we must go to.

An impromptu conversation with my dad years ago, apparently compelled me to think to be explicit in introducing myself when I am asked to introduce myself. I learnt to bring out my "PNA" in my introductions alongside few of my visible DNA features and traits. Sometimes the simplest questions are the trickiest to answer. One may spend their whole lifetime seeking an answer to an elementary question "who are you?". There are so many ways in which this question can be interpreted and responded to. The context is defined by who and why the question is being asked.

As I learnt this lesson, within a span of a few months later, it was in the school canteen; I had joined this new school reluctantly after we shifted home to another part of new Delhi. At Lunch, I shared a table with a few of my new classmates and one of them particularly seemed to be overly enthusiastic about my joining. At the very first moment of our eye-contact she asked me "Who are you?" blinking her eyes and biting into her grilled sandwich.

I instantly replied, "I am Priyanka Mehndiratta and your classmate." unaware she wanted a different response.

"I know that what I want to know is, who are you? Punjabi?". This was the definition of "who am I" redefined.

I nodded my head to confirm her guess and I could see a smirk on her face as she had successfully revealed a part of identity that I didn't consider vital to be mentioned. That was her James bond 007 moment.

Years later, after being asked this same question by so many people in different scenarios and words, I have gathered a more all-inclusive response to it. The utmost important fact to remember is that our names are nothing more than labels. I have various Indian spices in glass jars in my kitchen closet; neat labels are on these jars to identify them. That's exactly what our name does for us, identifies us! If I ask you to take these spice jars to someone who has never tasted or seen these spices and ask them to describe the taste and qualities of these spices, can they do it?

The answer is "No." A name on its own is not enough to describe our identity, our essence, or who we are. Just like the spices, we are much more than the labels.

We have our personal attributes, flavours, tastes, specific curries where these spices go well, and quantities in which these spices must be consumed. Sounds hilarious, but true. We need to go beyond the labels on the spice jars.

This is exactly what we all must do. Find out more about ourselves and go beyond the labels to decode our preferences. Who are the people who provide us comfort, whereas who are the ones who create discomfort for us? Do we enjoy any specific activities; what are our skills? What are we passionate about? As we start building a view of ourselves that goes beyond the names christened upon us, we will begin to enjoy our true self. The question arises: do we take time to identify our true self? Is it important to know your true self? I did spend a lot of time understanding the value I would get from it and, most importantly, how I can attain that knowledge. While browsing through a few articles on self-discovery the other day, I stumbled upon a quote-"Knowing Yourself is the beginning of true wisdom" by Aristotle, a renowned ancient Greek philosopher.

I could relate to it as I learnt through my experiences being self-aware and making efforts to discover one-self is an essential component of personal growth and intellectual development. As I focused on carving out time in my busy schedule for introspection and understanding my own strengths, weaknesses, and motivations, I felt confident in taking up challenges. The idea that true wisdom begins with a deep understanding of oneself is key to empowering ourselves with the right tools for various challenges we wish to take.

There were moments when I scratched my head to understand what's the difference between self and true-self. Am I not being true to myself? It took me a while to understand that in this world with disparate people, temperaments, cultures, languages and available choices, unknowingly, we adjust, compromises and long before we know, we lose touch with our authentic self. Our life experiences right from our early childhood create a version that might not be our true self. I could see different versions of myself as I grew up with time.

My personal experiences, education, and exposure built a different version of me with the passing years: a combination of my true self and acquired non-self-elements. Apparently, we all are a combination of different self and non-self-elements that we use in different combinations to address a situation at any point in time. Researchers have cited the importance of identifying the true self and how it adds to our self-esteem and makes our experiences more enjoyable in contrast to being connected to people or activities that utilise the non-self-elements of our personality. Humans, being social creatures, adopt various traits temporarily to fit in, although deep down it can impact our contentment.

As nature displays it, a complex process of metamorphosis transforms a caterpillar into a butterfly that can fly around. Similarly, we all go through the churn of time to become a multi-faceted personality. In my learning journey, I finished school in Delhi and flew to Mumbai to pursue higher education. Living alone in a different city culture further developed me as an individual, but what helped me stay happy was every time I connected back to my roots and my family home. A place where I could be my true self. This was my home, wherein I was accepted exactly the way I was, and it was okay to be imperfect. Many times, we are afraid of accepting our true self because we believe we are flawed. Our negative self-criticism takes over our intelligence and dictates that the true self is inferior. The reality is we are at our mental best when we are in connection with our true self. Be aware of who you are under these layers of social norms and labels. Make it a point to connect with yourself to understand who you are. Maybe it is a great idea to switch to the slam books that we had decades ago, wherein we used to fill in our friend's slam books to answer questions about our likes and dislikes. We will talk more about it in the following chapter, where we will dwell on the topic of - 'Listen to your inner voice.'

A walk down the memory lane reminds me of the famous 'Alice in Wonderland'- book by Lewis Carroll. Here is an excerpt of a conversation between Alice and Caterpillar from the book.

Who are YOU?" said the Caterpillar.

This was not an encouraging opening for a conversation. Alice replied rather shyly, "I–I hardly know, sir, just at present– at least I know who I WAS when I got up this morning, but I think I must have changed several times since then."

"What do you mean by that?" said the Caterpillar sternly. "Explain yourself!"

"I can't explain MYSELF, I'm afraid, sir." said Alice, "because I'm not myself, you see."

"I don't see," said the Caterpillar.

The truth is we all experience situations wherein we struggle to find an answer to a simple yet complex question "Who are you?". You don't have to look far to find an answer to it or wait for a caterpillar to ask you. It begins within all of us, we are the best judge of identifying, recognising and acting upon our true self. If we keep a record of our evolving needs, motivations, passions, likes and dislikes, we can keep up with our true self to fully enjoy our existence as a self-aware being. One must not rely solely on the external world to create an identity for them. The first step to getting an introduction to "Who we are?" begins with us being conscious of our needs, not letting them get diluted by the expectations imposed by others.

Here is a step-by-step guide for you to get started on your quest to explore your true self:

- Maintain a journal where-in you take notes on your dislikes and likes. Elaborate on these observations to identify which of these are more energy-draining tasks for you.
- As you take note of tasks that you like; Chalk out a plan how you can introduce more of these people, activities, sports etc. into your schedule.
- It is possible that your likings example: I absolutely love eating croissants, can be detrimental to your health or the stability in your life. Write a note in your journal to remind yourself that although it is your favourite or a preference, what are the reasons to keep it in a balanced quantity in your life. This will help you create a balance with who you are and a healthy, happy you.
- I would encourage you to read the book 'The Alchemist' by Paulo Coelho. The book talks about the journey of a young boy, who with each passing obstacle and hurdle adds valuable experience. In the process, he discovers himself too.

- Another recommendation for you is 'Wild: From Lost to Found on the Pacific Crest Trail', a memoir by the American writer, author, and podcaster Cheryl Strayed. An engaging read if you are new to 'self-discovery', the author takes its readers on an adventurous journey of her life. An amazing read on how she turns around her life after experiencing personal hardships. After numerous setbacks, Strayed decides to hike more than a thousand miles of the Pacific Crest Trail on her own. Through her honest and introspective storytelling, she reflects on her past and discovers inner strength and healing along the way. It's a captivating tale of adventure and self-discovery.

Self-discovery is rewarding for the soul; once you have discovered your true self, self-expression is a natural progression in this process. Self-expression can be as challenging as self-discovery. However, one may argue that "what is so complex about self-expression. if you know the answer to Who you are!". The obstacles in the path of self-expression are our fear of unacceptance by our loved ones or being deemed as a failure. To truly articulate ourselves once we are in tune with it takes a ton of courage to accept and endorse it even if we are not an instant success. It is a slow process with intense pressure from the outside world that turns you into a diamond, contrary to an ordinary stone. As you continue this journey, you transform yourself into a diamantaire who has mastered the skills to carve the "diamond of self-expression" further and emanate nothing but sheer radiance. A radiance of success and contentment of being in sync with your true self.

Before you get on to different ways one can adopt to express yourself, I would like to leave you with a beautiful quote to remind you to be brave to explore the outer world to know your inner self to build a connection that defines you.

"Don't be afraid to wander. Sometimes, getting lost is the best way to find yourself." – Paula Coelho, The Alchemist (1988)

Chapter 2
A Way to Express Yourself

A sweltering morning in Mumbai merged with the anxiety to perform well at the upcoming engineering college placement interview was ruinous. As I was getting ready hurriedly and competing for the limited resources at the hostel, my eyes welled with tears. Being a student in a working women's hostel made you powerless, and it was impossible to explain your urgency to fellow residents. With some luck and persistence, I managed to get ready for the 6:10 AM local train to get to my college in time for the placement interview. At the train station, even at the early hours, there was so much hubbub, and it was a battle on its own to get into the train and find a spot to stand. The loud chatters were piercing into my quest for a quiet. I tried hard to practise my answers to potential interview questions in my head. However, I was constantly interrupted by the memories of the comfort of my parent's home in New Delhi. At this very moment, I wanted to hug my parents tight and share my plight, relieving the burden on my heart. It was time to get out of the train, and effortlessly, I was pushed out onto the station like a big wave of sea hitting the shore.

In a fraction of a second, I had to gather myself to secure a ride in an auto rickshaw to make it on time to the college entrance before the gates were closed. Luckily, in another 5 minutes, I could squish myself onto the fourth seat in an auto, although I was unable to take out my notes to revise one last time. At that very moment, my mobile phone buzzed, and with great twisting and stretching, I received the call without noticing who was calling me.

"Hello dear, all the best for today! Don't worry, you are the best. How can someone miss a talent like you." My dad wished and assured me of my success on the phone call.

"Thank You, Dad. I will try my best." I replied hesitantly.

"Speak to your mom; she is excited, and your Satya aunty has sent her good luck wishes, too," Dad added and handed the phone to my mother.

"Priyanka, my dearest, you are my brave child. I am so proud of you already; you'll be the first one in your class to get placed. I can write it and give it to you right now. So go ahead and get it done. Speak soon. Lots of love from all of us here," Mum said excitedly, with total belief in my success.

I had to hold back my tears and hung up hurriedly. The last leg of my journey was a 5-minute walk, and as I lunged towards the entrance gates, I saw my Information Technology Professor, Mr. Chavan, taking count of the students who arrived and gave me a warm welcoming smile and said:

"Welcome, Priyanka! You are our best chance to secure a placement with this MNC, and you are our best candidate ever. Go ahead and smash it!"

I simply nodded and rushed inside. The day ended in 2 hours for me, while it lasted 9 hours for others. I was eliminated in round 1, aptitude test and wasn't surprised. As the aptitude test was handed over to us, the expectations from my parents and professor implored me to perform better, whereas I struggled to concentrate on solving any of the questions. I finished my exam without answering a single question. My other classmates stood out and waited with bated breath for their results. I was lost in my world, imagining myself spending time with my family back home in New Delhi and relishing their love. In the real world, a lot of people were taken aback by my failure in the first round and my failed opportunity to secure a job. I somehow felt relaxed and travelled back to my hostel to enjoy a quiet evening. My professors and parents were in greater disbelief than me and were eager to understand the reason for the failure of their very best. I assured them of a great performance in the next interview in line. However, that never happened. The trend seemed to continue for another three interviews, and finally, I gave up the act of being strong. The act of staying ignorant of my true emotions.

We all are busy living our lives and managing work, relationships, finances, and whatnot. Innately, we forget to connect with ourselves and fail to notice how we feel deep down. The process of ignoring our true emotions, feelings, and reactions, if continued for long, can be distressing. Subsequently, our connections with the outer world are impacted due to our misaligned internal state. It is a red flag to identify your true self. We aspire for successful personal and professional lives, but it becomes hard to clinch it without self-discovery combined with self-expression.

There is no single prescribed way to express ourselves, but we must discover it as we discover our identity. It started very early for me, at the age of 6, I found a way to connect with myself and express myself- writing was my answer. Being born in a family of working parents and three elder sisters, it wasn't a luxury to find peace and calm. Gradually, writing became a simple medium for me to express gratitude, love, and a surfeit of emotions within me. There were times in my fast-paced life, like my time at engineering college in Mumbai, when I deprioritised recording my thoughts and lost my connection with writing and myself.

Even though I had my "way to express" at my disposal, I was too busy to realise. I'm sure you'll not be surprised I continue to write to date to feel lighter and unfold my true self. I have friends who argue that it sounds like a cliché "Find your true self!". There should be a step-by-step guide available to help you achieve this. There is no forthright description well-known to enable us to connect with ourselves. However, there are a few principles that I gathered and believe can be imbibed to recognise ourselves from our own point of view. Here's what happened to me and how I explored ways to know 'Priyanka' better after I lost touch with my writing.

It was just after I passed college that I appeared for job interviews one after the other. Each time I appeared for the aptitude tests for the interviews, I felt my inner self was not in sync with what I was pursuing. I cleared the aptitude tests a few times when I tried hard to focus but failed in the interviews. The feeling of not belonging to the city, nostalgia, and indecision appeared in these interviews. Unknowingly, I presented myself as someone who has scored well in engineering but is not ready to accept a job yet.

Mustering courage, I had a very candid conversation with my family and confessed my homesickness and lack of strength to pursue a placement process at this time. It took a day for my dad to arrange for my train tickets and a week for me to get back home with all my belongings and bid goodbye to Mumbai. The feeling of being back in my home and lying in my bedroom doing nothing was surreal. There was so much comfort and warmth that I slept for long hours the first day after my arrival in Delhi. Nothing changed back home. Mom and dad continued bickering over tea, pulling each other's legs, while I enjoyed the home-cooked delicacies surrounded by love.

I spent the first few weeks sinking in the feeling of being back to my roots and how vivacious I felt around my family. In a matter of days, I began mulling over how I had missed opportunities to be employed. It was transforming into annoyance at my behavior as I constantly blamed myself for not being persistent enough and giving up too soon. The news of my college mates starting their employment in foreign countries and with reputed organisations was spreading like wildfire. Every time I received news like that, I could imagine myself getting that offer with ease if I had stayed in Mumbai for the interviews. "Why did I miss these opportunities?", "Why did I fail everyone?", " What does the future hold for me?" There were numerous questions haunting me all the time. I was losing my interest in eating, talking to my family, and for that matter to anyone." Why did I give up the golden opportunities?" was a question that was hitting me harder, as I was now done with the comfort of my home and proving my capability wrestled to become a priority in my head. Amidst the chaos, I had to find a way to do what I wanted to do and find out why I was running away from the opportunities presented.

It took me a few days to understand that I did secure an engineering degree in Information technology, but programming was not my sweet spot. I had to put immense effort into scoring well in my programming subjects and acting like a pro. The eureka moment has arrived; I was in a pressing need to connect with myself. For a long time, I emanated the expectations of the external world and considered myself a failure, wherein my real failure was to connect with myself to identify the true self hidden within me.

Now that I began actively engaging with my estranged self by spending time to pause and reflect on what I desire to be, I felt the need to actively express myself to articulate answers to the deafening sounds of self-doubt within me. A need to self-express and understand what 'Priyanka' wanted to achieve. I spent a lot of time exploring the various options I had to pursue my career post-engineering and start gauging my interests. I have a beautiful notebook, "My Guide" in my library that was my canvas for noting my thoughts and evaluating my options. I recorded my learnings from various conversations I had with my well-settled cousins and relatives. While I was exploring the career options, I decided to take an opportunity to work in different roles and understand my true calling.

I decided to step out of the industry and explore other available options that did not include software programming or testing. My first role was as an e-recruiter with a job search portal. It lasted a mere 20 days but stirred a lot of thoughts on what I wanted to achieve in my professional life. In this job, I had the simple task of logging into the database of available resumes to enter the keywords for the job requirement for the day. As a result of the process, the system returned a number of candidates resumes. It was an exciting first week, wherein

I enjoyed it like a kid who got access to Google search for the first time. By the end of the first week, the excitement evaporated away; I started questioning what I was doing with an engineering degree in Information Technology, an e-recruiter's job that could be done by anyone with basic search skills and the ability to follow instructions. I remember it was my 19th day at the job, and there was a total dissonance established in my mind about my role as a recruiter, my passion and my skill set.

The next day, the moment arrived when I decided to hand in my resignation with gratitude for the opportunity to discover what I was longing for. Not only that, it let me realise the value of my degree- the persistence of four years, my potential and it was pivotal for me to explore options where I can find a confluence of these two. I didn't want to choose a simple road just because it would be comfortable. I was in search of a role that offered me enough challenges to explore my highest potential, feel passionate about it and apply the knowledge I gathered in the past few years.

I missed the excitement of acquiring new and applying my existing knowledge in my first job. Thereafter, I continued my pursuit of a job that would make me feel excited about it and would offer an opportunity to upskill myself. A few days later, as I was trawling through the job portals, I discovered the role of a network engineer and their responsibilities. This started my period of preparation for network engineer interviews until I landed myself a job as a network engineer with a technology company to initiate my career. I excelled in the role and continued my career in the networking- and telecommunications industry for another 13 years. I understood myself better and finally had a job that was acceptable to my true self.

To everyone's surprise, who believed in me, I didn't secure a job through the engineering college placement process. I was uncertain and hopeless about what the future would hold. This self-discovery process took me to different points in my life, wherein I had to be brave enough as a 20-year-old to acknowledge that I didn't want to pursue a career that I had planned for.

Thanks to the crashing waves at the Worli Sea face in Mumbai that endured my questions and gave me strength unknowingly by their persistence to meet the shore. Kudos to my efforts to discover myself and my undeterred strength to slow down despite everyone around me speeding towards their professional best. The simple method of noting down my thoughts in 'My Guide' to spend time reading and reflect my inner debacles and aspirations cleared the way for me. The personal writings were so useful in identifying me and feeling more confident about my ulterior professional goal. In a few months, I could define "Who am I?", "What is my goal for the short-term, medium-term and long-term?", "What excites me in a job?". It gave me a feeling of transitioning to become a tour guide from a first-time visitor to a new city. Priyanka was discovered by herself and now it was time to express her true self.

How did I manage to discover and express my true self?

The key principle to connect with yourself is to find a way to let your inner self express it. Solitude is an incredible companion if used wisely, although it can be misconstrued as non-productive and literally being alone. Whereas it is our only opportunity to get to spend time in the company of ourselves. Centuries ago, the royals had allocated time to spend in solitude to introspect and connect. We, too, must pause, reflect, and take time with ourselves to explore our personal interests, be it painting, dancing, creative arts, writing, having conversations, cooking, gardening, and the list goes on if you want to get clarity in life make it a priority to spend time with yourself. I know one of my colleagues who ensures she is out for a 5K walk after a long day at work, especially when we end up sitting in our chairs in home offices. For me, a peaceful view of the fishes swimming in the pond, the greenery, a brisk walk, and a cup of tea are my go-to.

One more principle is the acceptance of your feelings, as you are aware of the feelings inside you, it gives you more control on the outside. It would be a lie if I asked you to stay positive and ignore your negative thoughts to be in control. One needs to accept the negative thoughts and go a step deeper inside to understand the root-cause of negativity to eliminate it. That's the only way you can understand what's going on inside and the attention required. Think of your life as a car. If your car is making a noise while you are driving it, will you stop to uncover the cause of the noise that's distracting you? Why will you not do the same in your life? Take a moment to hear your inner voice and act accordingly. With the advent of time, you will master the art of connecting with your inner self and will have a better answer to who you are!

The practice of Self-expression allowed me to communicate consistently with my thoughts, feelings, and opinions in a meaningful way, nurturing a deeper understanding of self and emotions within me. By solely engaging in creative activities like writing, scribbling with colours on a blank sheet or writing with a marker pen on a whiteboard led me to a more positive outlook in life. It improved my problem-solving and critical thinking skills and a deeper understanding of myself.

I have been encouraging my daughter to start her self-discovery and self-expression journey early to feel more confident about 'Who she is?'. She is super fond of sketching; painting and many times prefers to spend quiet time painting over the weekend. There was a short period wherein she stopped doing that and I could see her spending more time on her mobile phone. Without any surprise, there was an impact on her moods, temperament and behavior. I had to research on the internet to explain to her the various studies that have shown that self-expression in the arts positively affects mood, function, cognition, and behavior. Moreover, creative self-expression can substantially reduce stress, increase a sense of well-being, and promote resilience.

I managed to convince her and added furthermore to my knowledge base that finding a way to express ourselves plays a substantial role in developing our aptitude to relate to others emotionally and at the same time engage in deep relationships. I could vouch for it as merely, by integrating self-expression into my daily life by writing had led me to plentiful benefits, including appreciation for my existence, boosted my self-esteem, and enhanced the overall cognitive function of my brain (my personal observation:-)). Truly, by embracing a creative mindset and fostering an environment that encourages self-expression, anyone can unlock their full potential and experience personal growth.

Another principle to remember is to practice self-compassion. We've been taught from a young age to be compassionate towards others. With these deep-seated experiences, we forget to be kind to ourselves. Every individual has its own pace at which they progress and find their purpose. Stop being hard on yourselves and allow the voice within you to speak out loud.

There is no simple answer to "How can I discover myself and express myself too?". I have shared my journey to self-discovery and self-expression with you. In my story, my writing played a pivotal role in aiding me on my path to discovering my true self. This can be totally different for you. One of my friends at the Swimming Club, Liz and I, have discussed this topic at length and exchanged our personal journeys too. It was clear, for her, swimming played a crucial role in the whole process of self-discovery. Even today, swimming is her self-discovery tool. When in doubt, she goes for a swim to clear her head and connect with her inner self to look for answers.

I have also noticed if you are supported in your self-discovery journey by your loved ones, it becomes much easier to traverse the tricky paths to finding the right path that enlightens you and your passion. Here, I have shared a few steps that worked well for me when I used my writing as a tool to enable the self-discovery and expression process.

- So, do you have any ideas about how you will try and connect with yourself? I believe for me it is writing; I practise writing in a mindfulness journal wherein I can name my emotions for the day and collect my thoughts to reflect on how well I connected with myself.
- Do you find it difficult to express your true authentic views and ideas or do you envelop them with your non-authentic views to be heard?
- Have you tried expressing your emotions by writing a story, poem or painting on a blank canvas?
- It is a great opportunity to spend time with your loved ones on creative projects like gardening, decorating, painting your house, designing imaginary products, or simply sharing your wish list with each other.

As I started my own family, I have tried a few exercises with them to stay close to each other's true self. I used to have an exactly similar board just for myself. It didn't take me long to realise that it would be valuable to have a' Family Board'. It has helped me immensely to understand my growing daughter's feelings and clear my misconceptions about my spouse's emotions, too. As a family, we have clearly used it efficiently to understand each other and to respect our uniqueness. Well, we have taken the liberty to write for "Ferro" our pet dog, as he prefers playing fetch more than writing. Let me elaborate a bit more on the 'Family Board'.

- Our family has a weekly board that we use to communicate our likes and dislikes, it can be food, activities or an event that causes an emotional outburst. Certainly, this board is not hanging in the kitchen but a shared file amongst all four of us. Here is an example of what we include to encourage you to start one at your end too. It can be just for you or shared amongst your family; you get to decide.

	Priyanka	Pritam	Tanishka	Ferro (Dog)
I Love	'Day for Me'- Extra Holiday by my employer. -My new hair colors. -Lazy Mornings.	The new coconut curry I prepared.	Playing in the new Paddle Pool with Ferro. The Mangoes!	A limitless supply of the new treats-Crunch bites.
I Like	The new thriller series is super exciting.	Buying new plants and maintaining our garden. Long walks with Ferro- Trek this week was amazing!	-Learning French with Mom. -Swimming Disco with my friends last weekend.	Walking and sleeping all day long.
I dislike	Being sleep-deprived.	Arguing with the ladies at home!	Algebra is overpowering my brain!	Being alone at home while you go out shopping.
I despise	Arranging my wardrobe was dreadful!	Shopping all day long- like yesterday!	Encountering snails while I was gardening this week.	Houseflies hovering around me.

A very interesting story. One of the weeks, as I was caught up with stringent assignment delivery deadlines at work, I intentionally skipped updating the family board assuming, that no one would notice. It is just me who is super excited about it, so maybe I should let it go. To my surprise, I received a comment on our weekly board from my 10-year-old daughter stating, "Mumma, please fill in the family board for the week!!!!". This little nudge from my daughter really made me feel, it is not just for me but for her too. It was subtle feedback that it was working, and she enjoyed contributing as much as she awaited our inputs into it. I put a smile on my face. I parked everything that I was doing and ensured the board was up to date. Oh, I also added a comment to reply to her comment, "I love you Tanishka, thanks for reminding me. I am glad that you are enjoying it. Love Mom". The next thing that I remember is that she dashed into my study and gave me a big kiss on my cheeks with an excited "Love you Mommy!!".

Finally, just like writing, self-talk plays a crucial role in ushering you into the self-discovery process and then following through on it. In my study, right in front of my eyes, I have these lines to remind me not to forget the precious connection with my true self.

"The real treasure is inside you, exactly where you have hidden your true self."

Find your line to keep you on the path of self-discovery and expressing yourself as you are.

Chapter 3
Listen to Your Inner Voice

Have you ever visited a calm, serene place away from the hustle and bustle of the city and experienced the quiet? I had to wait for several years to get to a tranquil destination and absorb its serenity. It was first year of our marriage, and we visited my husband's village in Ratnagiri, Maharashtra in India. A perfect location with a stream flowing parallel to their ancestral house and dozens of Mango trees in the backyard. If we walked for a minute from there, we could see the paddy fields on both sides spreading all around us. The mornings were quiet, without human chatter or the noise of incessant honking by the traffic. The birds were the loudest and seized the mornings with their flamboyant presence and songs praising the beautiful mornings. Our morning strolls were so comforting; I could connect with nature seamlessly while I dwelled on the appreciation of our existence. Simply put, we were rejuvenating with nature by being aware of the presence of various natural beings and elements of the earth.

As we walked back to our home, I saw an old woman, most probably in her 80's, who was engrossed working in the paddy field with few other men and women. We waved at her, and she waved back with a big smile on her face. I walked up to her and appreciated how she was keeping her active. The conversation began and we chatted for another ten minutes sharing our happiness of being in the village.

She enquired, "Did you talk to yourself?"

We hesitated for a while, not sure what to reply.

"We've got each other to talk to. It is enjoyable," I giggled while I held my husband's hand.

"I have been doing it for my whole life. I meant the village is so calm in the mornings that you can hear your own heartbeat, rumbling stomach and your inner voice within you. It gives a lot of peace to talk without talking." She placed her hand on her heart as she explained what talking to yourself implied.

The next day, we went for a morning walk, enjoying the quiet around us while listening to our inner voice. A voice that is assured to be with us to achieve anything we wish to pursue in our lives. A voice that doesn't care about the inner critic but guides us to be open to the signs of nature and the universe, to receive and give from time to time.

I was learning to listen to my inner voice. There were numerous thoughts hovering in my mind, but the inner voice guided me on my course. After a couple of days, it was time to get back to the chaos of city life. I made it a habit to wake up and spend a few minutes in silence, staring out of the window at the green patch created by the mango trees in Mumbai. This became an integral part of my waking-up process. I had discovered an inner voice that encouraged me every morning to leave the comfort of my bed and chase my dreams.

With the advent of time, I advanced from a wife to a mother of a beautiful girl. Our daughter was almost 3 months old, and I received an interview call from a reputed firm that would accelerate my career progression. This was my golden ticket for getting into an MNC after moving to Mumbai after my marriage. The dilemma was how I could leave a young child and think about my career. There was all the assurance from my in-laws that if I was successful, they could take care of my daughter, and I mustn't worry.

I needed a talk. A conversation with my inner self as I had started doubting my capability as a mother, labelled myself as a selfish creature who is thinking of her career even though her child is so young.

"How can you do this, Priyanka? Why did you say yes to the interview in the first place?" My inner critic questioned my decision to go for an interview.

"I never thought you could be so selfish. Just look at your daughter's face, she is so tiny and needs you". The inner critic continued patronising me.

Tears rolled down my cheeks as I contemplated what to do.

My husband supported my decision of getting back to work and encouraged me. However, the inner critic's opinion was overwhelming me causing a state of indecisiveness.

The next morning, I started my day with the same ritual of trying to connect with nature by looking out of my window in peace as everyone slept. I heard a whisper from within

"Do not fear, you are not wrong in pursuing your dreams when you have the right support. The choice to work cannot diminish your love for your child." A strong opinion wrapped with a motherly comfort assured me of my intention to get a new job.

I did go for the interview the next week, but before I left, I held my daughter in my arms and whispered in her ear, "Mom is going for a job interview. Wish me luck. Don't trouble grandma; I will be home in 2-3 hours".

The interview was successful, so I rushed home to see my daughter. To my surprise, my daughter slept all afternoon peacefully and as soon as I entered home, she woke up with a loud cry.

Now my strength and belief in my inner voice was getting deeper. Yes, I took up the new job and we all raised our daughter as a family responsibility and treasure.

I still wonder if I had ignored those tiny whispers within me, I might have been on a different trajectory altogether or living with regrets for not taking the opportunity when it knocked at my door. Even after I made my decision, starting the new job wasn't easy, as I faced challenges working in a male-dominated industry, an inflexible work culture, and being underestimated just because I was a young mother. It was, once again, my inner voice every single day that taught me persistence and not to be a victim of others' opinions about me. The daily reminder of why I am at work in the first place—for a better future for my daughter and a best-in-class education—kept me going as I continued to pave the path for my corporate succession.

It was hard work to learn to tune in to my inner voice, a voice that would guide me towards my aspirations. Probably, I was surrounded by lots of voices with different opinions and a transactional life took away my opportunities. It took me a while to differentiate between the inner critic and the inner voice. I had to turn down the volume of my inner critic to hear what my inner voice was saying to me. I believe it is perfectly alright, if you are in a similar situation struggling to listen to your inner voice. Imagine being in a busy market filled with cacophony of noise from vehicles, street vendors and passersby. The noise levels are tumultuous, making it impossible to listen to the person walking with you. What would you do if you had something important to say right there? Going a bit closer to their ear might help, right? Let's change the situation a little bit; what if you wish to connect to your inner self amidst this chaos? Is it possible? Well, not easy. To hear your inner self, you must go deeper and turn down the noise around you.

Here are a few steps you can take to cut through the everyday noise and hectic schedules and develop a deeper relationship with your inner voice.

- Practise mindfulness: Create a space for yourself throughout the day to have a thinking space. Eat mindfully to include mindfulness as an integral part of your daily routine. For instance, we tend to eat more when we are not conscious of our eating, and our senses are focused on other external activities like watching television. Next time you eat, pay attention to colours, smells, tastes, texture and consistency. Similarly, you can take this practice to other activities, be in the present and enjoy the existing engagement.
- There are many voices in your head, just like a radio. Find your frequency and tune into it. This needs practice in listening in rather than listening out.
- Start by being a better listener on the outside. When in team meetings or having a conversation with your child, be patient and listen to them calmly without rushing to speak back. The listening skill on the outside will enhance your listening inside skill, too.

- Self-care is pivotal to connecting with your inner voice. Remember, it is your inner voice, and you must take care of yourself as a starting point to connect deeper with it. Take care to be heard. Mental and physical health must be a priority, and they go hand in hand.
- Pay attention to your surroundings and the people around you.
- Practice mindfulness—start writing in a mindfulness journal. As you write and silently read, you develop a connection with your inner voice.
- Don't pressurise yourself to hear your inner voice. Create an environment where you can do a tech detox or feel your existence. Pay attention to your hands, the shape of your feet, the colour of the grass in the garden, the new blooms of the season, the budding wildlife in the pond, and the flowering fruits. This act of consciously acknowledging your own presence and appreciation for nature will nurture an environment to hear the inner voice monologue.

The inner voice can be feeble or overpowered by other voices in your head; the voices that you hear because of other's opinions about you. The onus lies on you to take time to find your inner voice and build a strong connection with it forever.

As Steve Jobs, founder of Apple, said: "Don't let the noise of other's opinions drown out your own inner voice."

– Steve Jobs

Chapter 4
Acknowledge Your Fears

Six months had passed in our new home, and we were now feeling settled there. We had made plans for home improvements while we were busy making the home ours with a couple of changes in the décor. Everything seemed to go perfectly, except I had something eating me from inside. Pritam and Tanishka were flying to India for a week, as it would be her summer holiday, while someone had to stay with Ferro in the UK. Moreover, I had a key project that was ongoing that didn't permit me to go on holiday because of approaching deadlines. There was a discomfort in staying alone in a house that was quite big for me and Ferro to be on our own.

I had a few plans in my head about how I would manage myself during that week. Worries continued to grow within me while it was the day of their flight to India. We bid goodbye to each other, and reality struck. "I was afraid of living alone, I am scared of the dark; I can't go out in the garden to relieve Ferro during nighttime; I was also afraid of the quiet". This made me think how can a self-discovery and a self-expression journey be complete without acknowledging our fears. Fear has been associated with negative feelings, but it is a healthy emotion. The trouble lies in our efforts to suppress the fears within us and imagine endless possibilities. This profound thought took me back to the time when I was about to join the engineering college in Mumbai, ignorant of my fears. I vividly remember my feelings the night before I set out on a journey to build educational excellence for myself; here is what happened that night.

The glistening moon on a rainy night in the month of August was preceded by a busy day with my best friend Ananya, sisters visiting me with good luck gifts, and packing my bags for travel the next morning. Ananya was disappointed with my decision to leave biochemistry to join engineering as she despised mathematics. Her dislike for mathematics grew after I chose engineering over our friendship for many years. Reluctantly, she came home with a handmade greeting card that read- "Good Luck!" her visit was brief but left me heavy-hearted as I would miss her friendship. I hoped that I might see her during my next visit back home.

The day slipped through quickly like the sand through our fists. Words of encouragement were offered to me every now and then by my sisters, whereas my young nieces probed my decision to go away from Delhi. It was impossible to sleep that night as the raindrops constantly pattered on my window reminding me of a new start, as I lay on my bed with eyes wide open. The darkness of the night was nothing compared to my fears, and I felt overwhelmed with emotions of excitement, sorrow and disbelief. It was my last night in the comfort of my parental home before I moved to Mumbai from Delhi to start my engineering studies. I tossed and turned in my bed, frightened by the thought of being on my own and away from the warmth, support and constant chatter of the family. The fears were playing on a loop inside me and imagined the worst.

In my imaginary world, I could see myself lost in the busy streets of Mumbai and crying for help. As if it wasn't scary enough, I imagined being kicked out of the college by the Engineering College Principal, Mr. Deshpande has his face fumed with rage. The negative thoughts spiraled endlessly until I got up from my bed to get a glass of water. I didn't sleep that night as I was constantly battling to escape these natural thoughts. The cycle of these negative thoughts presented into a dream continued even after I finished college, missed my placements and returned to the comfort of my home. I would dream of securing a perfect job just on the day of joining, I wouldn't get any transport to get to the office. I started having so many dreams that it was difficult to differentiate between dreams and reality. It became a norm in the family wherein I would share my adventurous Alice in Wonderland dreams with my parents to be reminded to not to overthink.

"Pichu, you are over thinking about the placements, you will get a job. If you'll not get, who will get a job? Tell me." My forever positive mum responded to my catastrophic dreams of failure to get a job or to get to work after securing it.

"Mom is right, think of positive things before sleeping and chant *Hanuman Chalisa.* You will be fine" Dad assured me of the solution.

Well, days turned into months and years as I progressed in my self-discovery journey along with a way to express myself; there was one clear realisation- I cannot ignore my fear. I must acknowledge and befriend them. During the early phases of my self-discovery, I was unable to acknowledge my fears. Maybe I wasn't mature enough to understand it. Today, I plainly have a clear list of what I am fearful of, and as I conquer them, I keep updating them to know what stops me from experiencing or moving ahead in life. What are those fears that can stand in the way of happiness for my family and me, or can I find a way with them on my side?

Alright, before you start making a mental list of what you are fearful of, let me share something I stumbled upon on YouTube, an inspiring story about Franklin D. Roosevelt (FDR) and his inaugural speech. The excerpt from the speech is – 'Only thing we have to be afraid of is the fear itself'- Roosevelt's famous twenty-minute inaugural speech in 1933 after he accepted the nomination of the Democratic party. He stood with great courage and conviction on the stage, outlining the New Deal (a plan) to bring America out of the Great Depression. His audience on the day, the Americans who were experiencing the constant threat of an increasing unemployment rate and were dejected by the inaction of the previous government.

It was brave to propose a new plan to an assembly who has lost their trust in the government and was filled with anguish was not a cakewalk! Do you think FDR was afraid when he stood there? Possibly yes! The victory is in the fact that he overcame that emotion and successfully delivered the message. Understand fear, it is a by-product of our overthinking when we are anxious about an expected outcome based on our efforts. The anxiety about the uncertainty leads us to anguish and when anguish overpowers us, we are disoriented. How powerful and simple this chance encounter changed my attitude from surrendering to my fears to making an effort to get past them by acknowledging them wholeheartedly.

The challenge is that fear comes in different shapes and forms, healthy and unhealthy too. Healthy fear if it acts as a warning for us with the least impact on our life, and unhealthy if it inhibits our ability to grow in our lives. Fears can hide within us to be unseen by the naked eye and blend completely in our behavior. I recall my first attempt at swimming in the pool with a friend. We both were confident that I would swim naturally. Instead, I panicked as soon as I felt the depth of the water to be pulled out to safety. That's how my fear of water began. It was so strong that I was afraid to see a loved one going for a swim. I couldn't live with this fear for life, I had to find the courage to get past it. I did it eventually at the age of 36, when I decided to learn swimming. Rewind, I had moved to the UK from India by my employer to be closer to our enterprise clients. When I went in to enroll my 7-year-old daughter for swimming, something sparked within me, and I blurted at the receptionist of the leisure club, "Do you have swimming lessons for adults, too?".

She responded firmly, "Yes, we do. Are you looking to enroll?"

That's how I got myself enrolled in adult swimming lessons. On the day of my first lesson, when I entered the swimming pool area, I could see and hear loads of younger kids splashing and swimming with confidence. In fact, the youngest one might have been less than a year old and was swimming with his mom. I had to have a self-talk to continue walking toward my swimming instructor. The swimming journey had begun by now. It was not just the fear of water but the strange feeling of wearing a swimsuit, taking a shower before dipping in the pool. All of it was so odd and unusual at the same time for me.

During the first few lessons, I was conscious about how I looked, and if everyone was watching me. My mind was boggled, wondering why, even after kicking, I was not moving forward. I was grappled by the fear that the moment I stopped kicking, I would drown in the pool. A swimming pool that was 1.3 meters deep, whereas I am almost 1.67 meters tall. It took me a few lessons to understand that the best way to move forward was to streamline the body, keep going, kick slowly, and stay calm. Don't we all feel that in life sometimes, that even after working hard, we are stuck in the same place? Nevertheless, the answer is in acknowledging the fear, staying calm, continuing to kick, learning to breathe underwater every now and then, and you'll move ahead eventually. Sorry, did I just answer how to swim and survive?

Great news for me and my loved ones is that we all can now happily swim. Our childhood experiences and exposures are the foundations of our fear that get carried over the years and need effort to overpower them. A precarious situation sensed by our brain that has a physical, emotional, or psychological impact ultimately leads to fear. When I was back in school, I had stage fright, which was discovered when I stepped on the stage for the first time. I froze on the school stage. However, the regular opportunities in the school, from reciting nursery rhymes to reading the news headlines in the morning assembly, slowly aided in my fight with stage fright. Within a few years, my teachers identified my capability as an orator that could be worked upon; consequently, I participated and won accolades for my school in various debate competitions. By the time it was my last year in school, I was president of the debates club, mentoring other students to get over their stage fright and participate in such events.

It was as if I had discovered a winning recipe for debate competitions, etc. The stage was no more a demon but a partner in crime. The acknowledgement of my fears at an early age ensured I paved the path for my success as a speaker by working towards befriending them. I couldn't have done this on my own. In both my pursuits to get over my fear of stage and water, I was supported by my will, a guide- teacher or instructor and the discipline to take a small step towards it.

A long time back, when I was working as a technical trainer with a telecommunications organisation, it was the early years of my career. Essentially, I was learning on the job. Conversely, the training courses I delivered on various technical topics were attended by experienced individuals, and a few of them were hands-on with these technology fundamentals more than I knew. Every single day, when I had my training in the diary, a battle went on within me. Self-doubt crept in and was thrashed by my confidence. As I waited on the day of training for the trainees to join, the anxiety was evident on my face, and I felt the fear of failure or fear of not knowing the answer to something mounting. I wasn't going into these training sessions but entering a battlefield. I prepared beforehand, focused on the topics, discussed with my peers, and took notes from every training session that I delivered. In a short time, I had expanded on my knowledge base, the types of questions that would be asked, topics I needed to explain better, and so on.

From day 1 of my first-ever training session to the 10th training session I delivered, I had started believing in myself, and there was no more fear. The reality is, if there is fire, smoke will be around. If you want to experience something new, there will be anxiety. The whole process taught me to accept my fears and find a way out of them. Looking back, those early days of facing my fears as a technical trainer were a profound learning experience.

These experiences taught me that bravery isn't the absence of fear but the willingness to confront it. Winston Churchill once said," Fear is a reaction, and courage is action." I had many reactions to various situations, organisms, people, and so on. What I needed the most was action in the form of courage to befriend these fears. This statement from Churchill resonated completely with my desire to win over these fears to achieve my aspirations.

Years later, it took me a lot of courage to accept a position in a new country and leave my six-year-old daughter Tanishka back in India. My personal fear of losing my parents triggered the fear of Tanishka feeling shattered without her mother by her side. I was going berserk, imagining the worst. What if I am asked to leave after a year of my move? What if Tanishka is unable to fit in? How will I connect with my parents? In fact, the impostor syndrome kicked in, and I questioned my ability to work at the global headquarters of the MNC, which has so many responsibilities.

Now was the time to acknowledge my fears and befriend them. I had to understand my trepidations that were in my way of securing a better prospect. My husband had to remind me of his caring nature, and he would have his parents taking care of our daughter. I reminded myself, why must I take this opportunity? Certainly, I wished to give my daughter Tanishka greater exposure to opportunities to grow and, at the same time, use this move as a launchpad for myself. After searching deep within myself for the courage to make it happen for her, everything added up alright as I kept my calm and trusted the support system I had around me. See, you can do it! The more you understand your fear, the better your response will be, and slowly you can befriend them.

We all experience a variety of fears, such as losing our power, position, love, health, friends, favorite things, people, and, lastly, our life. By living within the boundaries created by fear, we forget to cherish this one chance to live. We deny ourselves the best views, people, relationships, knowledge, feelings, and so much more. Having said that, if the greatest explorers, scientists, and discoverers had lived their lives in fear, the world today would be a very different place. Have you ever thought of your trepidations that impede you from being successful?

If you do, it's time to acknowledge those fears and overcome them. Another exercise that we practice at home is a 3-step Fear Drill exercise that allows you to focus on one of your fears. I designed this exercise years ago when my list of fears was long, and after prioritisation, we managed to focus on one of them—Fear of Water. I realised even after living in the UK, I was unable to enjoy the beautiful beaches due to my fear of water. I was constantly caught by the thought of drowning. I simply acknowledged it and took a step towards overcoming it by learning swimming and going swimming every week.

Exercise: A 3-step Fear Drill exercise for you:

Make a list of the top 5 fears that you believe stand in the way of your professional growth, a healthy lifestyle, and being yourself. These can be any fear that you believe, if removed from your life can build a better version of you. All you need is a pen, paper and pause for reflection.

Take some time out of your busy schedule to imagine how they impact your life today and what will change if you can successfully overcome them. Pick your top 3 fears from your answer and make a note of how you can overcome it. Here is a quick glimpse of how I try to take a note of my top fears and think of ways to overcome them.

Top Fears	Impact	Overcome – How?
Fear of Spiders.	Negligible	
Fear of Water.	High Impact	Take: Swimming Lessons- Before Summer I need to learn swimming.
Fear of being outdated	High Impact	
Fear of Failure in tasks assigned.	Moderate	
Fear of sharing honest feedback.	Moderate	

Every time I feel overwhelmed by fear, I close my eyes and tell myself, fear will haunt you if you do not act upon it. Will you act upon it?

Well, if you have decided to act upon it, you have conquered the first step of befriending your fears. Yes, you heard it right; the best way to go beyond the boundaries set by your fears is to acknowledge them and befriend them. Like in my personal experience, I had to act on them to create a bond with them and befriend them. It took immense effort to progress them from the unhealthy to the healthy category of fears. You can develop a method to take these baby steps to acknowledge them, followed by identifying if they are causing high impact (unhealthy) or little impact (healthy). Once you have this, gather the courage within you to take your first step toward them.

Learning from my experience, I have developed a simple process for processing my fears and ultimately befriending them.

- **Is your fear real?** Take time to contemplate the root cause of your fear. Is it related to your personal experience, hearsay or is it the uncertainty around a situation, individual, place, activity or anything that is driving the fear within you?

- **Go a step further**: Assess your what-if and how questions. Ask yourself what will happen if your fears are valid. If you doubt your capabilities, look at your past performance. Look for that reason: why would someone entrust you with something if you are not good at it?
- **Imagine your life without fear:** This one is a masterstroke. Imagine yourself living without the fear that is holding you back from enjoying life. I imagined myself living in a beautiful city in the UK with my family and big smiles on my family members' faces. I love dogs, so I spiced up my imagination with a family pet as a new addition to our family. This gave me another reason to overcome my fears and befriend them.
- **Be a better version of yourself:** It is always motivating to think of how I can be a better version of myself by befriending my fears.
- **Don't ignore ignorance:** Sometimes real facts help us in deciding if the fears that we own are real? What is the probability of the fear happening in reality? It is simply ignorance on certain aspects that remains uncovered for years decorated by our fears for life. Try to acquire knowledge to enlighten the dark lanes of fear, it will help you pave your way to a brighter space. Ultimately, fear is ours to face, and only we have the power to free ourselves from its grip. By becoming aware of the fears that hold us back, we can seek help in different ways and, over time, learn to overcome them and grow beyond them.

Chapter 5
Who is Your Mirror?

I love mirrors! They are so authentic and aesthetic. That's one of the reasons why we were looking for a mirror for our new home. My spouse, Pritam, and I wandered from one store to another to find a mirror that could be the latest addition to our living room. I had imagined an elaborate bronze frame with intricate carvings outlining. The mirror is sizable enough to cover most of the wall behind our dining table. The idea to have a mirror exactly on that wall was to be able to see the reflection of our garden right across it, through the living room's large windows.

After a long search in various furniture stores, we decided to check in a charity store. The mirror we were after was right there on the display. How did we miss it? As I sought it from the outside through the glass walls of the store, I could see a happy reflection of me admiring the beauty of this timeless piece. The bronze carvings of birds and flowers with a delicate touch of fine black lines to accentuate the infinitesimal features were beguiling. Suddenly, I felt so much love for myself as I looked at my silhouette in the mirror. Once again, after a long time, I cherished looking and acknowledging who I am. My gaze was stuck on it and I was lost in admiring it and how it emanated energies to venerate me.

Pritam enquired. "What do you think of it? I kind of like it," he asked intriguingly.

"Let's get it before it is gone!" I rushed into the store before someone else claimed it.

I excitedly enquired if it was still available from the lady at the cash desk, and she nodded to confirm. Chuffed with her response, I gave a thumbs up to Pritam to confirm our feat in the quest for a mirror for our home. The next evening, we had the mirror hanging on the living room's wall, strikingly reflecting the lush green garden in it. The garden looked equally picturesque in the mirror; the only difference was the wall was blessed with a new life.

Mirrors are great additions to a living space, brightening the space if positioned correctly. They enable us to experience beauty in simple things that are otherwise ignored. The wall seemed lifeless, and today, the wall seemed to celebrate the presence of a mirror that could reflect whatever we presented to it. It was no more monochrome but had the power of the mirror to give it colours, adding to its beauty and grandeur. The mirror reminds us of the fact that change is inevitable. It is a symbol of the impermanence of beauty and the world. I recall when my own daughter, Tanishka, as an infant, saw a mirror. She laughed hysterically and played with her own reflection, thinking she had met a friend. It took her some time to realise it was Tanishka on the other side, too. She happily pointed at herself and the mirror, exclaiming, "Tanu!".

Our pet dog, Ferro, as a puppy, barked at his own reflection in the mirror thinking another dog had intruded on his space. With the advent of time, he understood and accepted the company of a similar looking dog in the mirror. When it comes to adults, we tend to look in the mirror every day. However, we unknowingly distance ourselves from this gaze, only rarely connecting with that reflection in the mirror - that is perhaps the rush of thrill I felt when I observed myself in the mirror at the Charity shop. Such is the sublime power of simple yet powerful mirrors; by making a conscious effort, we could use the power of mirrors effectively to take a step towards our self-discovery and improvement. Having realised the power of mirrors, I wouldn't question why great philosophers associated mirrors with thought. Essentially it is a mental instrument that is the reflection of the universe and enables you to observe yourself.

Plato's Allegory of the Cave comes to mind, where prisoners mistake shadows for reality until one escapes and sees the world in its true form. Similarly, mirrors help us see beyond mere reflections to the essence of who we are. Like the escaped prisoners, we must seek mentors and self-awareness to understand our true selves. Even Lacan's mirror stage theory, though modern, sheds light on the profound moment of self-recognition. A small object with great depth and wisdom. It would be unfair not to mention Socrates' view on self-reflection - "An unexamined life is not worth living." A mirror reminds us of time after time about the power of self-reflection in our lives.

Nowadays, it is common for us to hide behind the filters available in social media applications and refuse to accept our true identities. We switch from one filter to another, changing our view of how we look or who we are. On the contrary, these mirrors do not hide anything from us and show us our identity. They reflect our true emotions, our scars on the inside and the outside without any filters. We can see ourselves transform our looks from the time we wake up to when we get ready for work. It is a subtle reminder for us to transform similarly but on the inside. Who can be that mirror for you? What can an ordinary mirror not do? Metaphorically, these are our mentors or our loved ones who care enough to help us understand and develop our own identity. An identity that goes beyond the physical looks and peeks deeper into making us better human beings in our personal and professional lives.

I had a very candid conversation with Phil, one of the trainers of a soft-skills programme sponsored by my organisation. I questioned him that every time I ask my colleagues for feedback, they shower me with appreciation for my work and skills. However, I am conscious that I need continuous improvement to be better and future relevant too.

"It seems impossible to find someone who can show me a mirror. It could be so much easier, if I get an understanding of how I am perceived in the team. What changes I must apply to my behaviour to be a better version of myself" I seethed with a genuine frustration of inability to get an acknowledgement of improvement areas for myself.

"It is not easy to get critical feedback from someone. It is a skill; you must extract it. Not everyone can share the feedback easily as they are apprehensive of hurting your feelings" Phil explained with confidence.

"You need a mirror; find a mentor first with whom you build a connection so that they feel comfortable to show you the mirror. You must show them that you are receptive to it and will not let the mentor-mentee relationship be impacted. Once you find such a mentor, don't let them go. However, you need more of these mirrors' aka mentors. Build your network of Mentors who can keep you honest and guide you". Phil explained with an ease exalted by his experience of several years.

It made me ponder the value of mentors and how mirrors resonate with the clarity one could get from a mentor. Mirrors are such an integral part of our lives, and when placed in the right location, they can be of great value. Think of the rearview and side mirrors in a car—they must be adjusted correctly to get a clear view and drive safely. When I started learning to drive a car in the UK, one of the first things I learned was to do a 5-point check before moving off in my car. However, I struggled to keep up with it as I would rush to move out of the car. Each time, my driving instructor, Teresa, patiently explained the process to me, doubting my ability to learn to drive in my mid-thirties.

"You need to do 5-point checks before and after selecting gear: Check the left blind spot, left mirror, middle mirror, right mirror, and right blind spot (5 points). Select gear."

Repeat the 5 points check again. You can fail your driving test for missing the mirrors" She looked into my eyes to ensure I was following her instructions as she pointed with her hands the 5-points to be checked.

"You know it is not just to pass the driving exam but to ensure safety for you and anyone on the road to avoid surprises. What would you do if you moved off without checking your mirrors and there was a speeding car coming from behind?" Teresa emphasised the importance of the mirrors. It took me a few classes before I mastered the 5-point check, and it occurred to me naturally to make sure I was checking the mirrors.

I believe such is the importance of individuals who can be mirrors in our lives. These individuals can guide us on our journey so that we can prepare ourselves before we head on our quest for success. Simply put, we all need guides, mentors, and coaches in our lives who can give us critical feedback. The major challenge that I had in my career was that there was a lot of appreciation but little progress. I was getting frustrated. How is that possible? If I am great at what I do, then why am I not being considered for a promotion? It made me hungry for critical feedback and a search for people who can show me the areas I need to improve on.

Thanks to Phil's guidance, I found great mentors who became my mirrors and gave me the key to becoming a better version of myself. I started building a picture of my strengths, my weaknesses and how I can use my strengths to overpower my weaknesses. It is not easy to get critical feedback, it takes courage to receive feedback prudently and then act on it. If you will act defensive while receiving the feedback, you will end up shattering your mirror and your opportunity to flourish.

Just as my mentors helped me through my career, we all need mirrors to reflect our true selves, revealing both our strengths and areas for improvement. This concept of mirrors reminds me of a story from my childhood that beautifully brings out the power of honest reflection. Let's roll back to our younger days when story time was an exciting time. I would insist my mother tell a story so that I could go to sleep. The Story of Snow White and the seven dwarfs is a great example of how the wicked queen was so lost in her quest to be the most beautiful woman that she espoused a brutal resolution to achieve it.

Even her mirror was honest and couldn't hide the reality of Snow White's enviable beauty. Evidently, she didn't use the mirror for the right things or couldn't accept the reality shown by the mirror and lost her mind in utter indignation. Snow white was kind to the seven dwarfs and grateful for giving her a place to hide. As a result, when Snow white was in need, it was her Dwarf friends who took good care of her! In the end, the choice is ours, whether we want to feed ourselves with ego or be kind. The mirror spoke nothing but the truth to the evil queen, although the queen decided to stay blinded by her belief in supremacy.

A mirror is so multi-faceted; it can do so many things for so many different people, yielding results aligned to their requirements. For the evil queen, it was a measure of perfection or physical beauty, whereas for a scientist, it is an object that reflects light. We can derive something from a mirror, too. If you understand the mirror's value, it is the best self-reflection tool at your disposal. I have heard a saying: how do you face yourself in the mirror after your wrong deeds? The mirror knows it all—your secrets and you. It is your constant aide-mémoire to be true to yourself, believe in yourself, and tell yourself during tough times that this too shall pass. It will be with you during your good times to keep you grounded. A mirror imparts the confidence to look right into everyone's eyes and express your views, to find your own voice. It is important that we do not forget who we truly are and accept all our imperfections. Here are a few exercises that I have used time and again to make the mirror my friend who is true to me:

- It is fantastic to stand in front of the mirror every morning and affirm, "I am not less, not more than anyone. I am enough to do right and spread goodness wherever I go. I am a wonderful creation with unlimited capabilities. I accept my authentic self as I am while I continue to develop harmony between my mind, soul, and body!
- Next time you have that important speech to inspire your audience, don't miss practising it in front of the mirror. A speech is not just a combination of words but an amalgamation of expressions, tone, hand movements and words!
- Mirrors remind you of your health and emotions that you are feeling. Use the mirrors perfectly to look at yourself without the filters to read your true emotions and signs of healthy mind and body.
- Take time to clean the mirrors in your home, sometimes, it is required to see a clear view of yourself.
- Experiments with different backgrounds and lights with the mirrors in your home to enable them to reflect the mood you wish to tune into.
- Look into the mirror together with your loved ones to derive the simple pleasure of companionship or to celebrate a great partnership.
- Use your time with your mentors wisely by asking them questions that can give you a generic view of what best looks like and then work with them on how you can be the very best.

- Do not hide your thoughts or feelings from mentors. Would you hide your face and look in the mirror to see how you look? It is crucial to be honest with your mentors to allow them to help you in your journey of self-discovery and success.

Remember, nothing is perfect, and always striving to be perfect might make you forget the essence of your true self. Be yourself, step out without makeup, in your favourite PJs, with stubble and a clumsy look, but don't forget to wear a smile. Lastly, say thanks to the mirror for keeping you honest and a mantra to live by—a beautiful person is one who can look into the mirror, accept the imperfections, and continue to spread happiness and kindness.

Chapter 6
Identify the Weeds Around You

Time flies. When I look back, there was a moment when I was deliberating, as a young mother, whether to accept a new job opportunity while my daughter was just under 3 months old, and I ultimately did join them. Instead of welcoming me, many of my colleagues challenged my decision to be back at work too soon, with my daughter still semi-dependent on me for her meals. It was an emotionally rough period, even though it was a well-thought-out decision, and my daughter was in the good care of her grandparents. Such brazen comments depleted me of my desire to achieve more. The first few days at work were arduous, as I had a feeding schedule for my daughter, and the human body gets trained to it. Not having my daughter around at those times made it physically difficult for me, too.

As a young mother of a first child, there was a lot more to learn than I had acknowledged. With each passing day, I was improvising in managing myself emotionally and physically. A continual reminder of the greater cause of why I am out here working in the first place sharpened me to shift my thoughts from disapproval to a sense of achievement. Simple, age-old tactics were my friends, I avoided having more than essential conversations with people who imposed their opinions on me and deprived me of my energy resources. At the same time, I found few colleagues who supported me simply by not questioning my decision to rejoin work after a brief maternity break. They simply treated me just like any other engineer; appreciated my presence in the team for my skills and appreciated my contributions. They became my source of energy to continue in my new role. I didn't feel the guilt anymore; learning new skills every day made me a different person. A great day at work, followed by a burst of enthusiasm to hold my daughter in my arms after work created a perfect aplomb. The choice I made was attributing towards my success, a choice to focus on positive influences and filter the negative ones. I had to simply think of myself as the captain of the cricket Team who is clear about what she wants to achieve in a cricket match: a win for her team. It doesn't matter to the captain what negative influences dictate but all she does is to keep driving herself and her team towards victory.

With a blink of an eye, two years passed by, and I realised the need to look for other opportunities with more potential to learn and grow. It was the rise of ambitious Priyanka taking control of herself and her aspirations besides motherhood. I reminisce how slowly I was transforming into a woman who could play many roles alongside her job, filled with aspirations to continually grow. I applied and interviewed for quite a few roles outside of my organisation at that time before I got selected at a major Telco company to work as a Pre-sales Architect for Large Enterprise Accounts. It seemed to be a breakthrough in my career after a long time. Maternity did slow me down, and I had knowingly accepted the comfort zone in my previous role several times. The transition to a new organisational role meant stepping out of my comfort zone to challenge myself as a technical salesperson for the first time ever. All this while, I enjoyed being an engineer behind a screen, although now I would be front-ending conversations with leading enterprise accounts with global presence. A new beginning with new challenges with a young child—once again, there were many who stopped me before this transition. Fortuitously, I had great support from my family, and these negative voices could be suppressed.

Fortune didn't seem to last long. I received a warm welcome from everyone at my new organisation except one. It didn't bother me as Esha was the only one. The challenge was I didn't realise Esha would play a crucial role in my job. Seemingly, she had to hand over a few of her accounts to me, as I was an addition to an existing team to share the load of numerous large accounts. In our first team meeting with our manager George, wherein he proposed the plan to divide the accounts amongst a couple of us, Esha completely rebelled against the idea and erupted, "Why do we need to give her our accounts?" while she rushed out of the meeting room. It left all of us uncomfortable to continue our meeting, and me the most.

With a hope that this too shall pass, I looked forward to another day at work. Finally, the accounts were divided amongst us, and I contacted her to get the handover notes and documents for these accounts. Ostensibly, whatever I tried wasn't working well, and I received cold responses to my requests, or I was completely ignored. It started taking a toll on my mental health as I was unable to get through to her. George intervened a couple of times, and all of it made me uncomfortable. She succeeded, and I gave up. I walked up to our manager, bursting into tears, stating, "Why did you hire me? There is no point working!" Another manager, Martin, who overheard us, intervened and apologised for interrupting our conversation and offered that I could join his team instead. My head was spinning, burdened with the thought of, "Was my decision right, to take up this role?"

"You are not going anywhere. Leave it to me, you will have everything you need to be successful in your role," George assured me.

The thoughts of facing or working with Esha were draining my energy, and I realised this could not last long. I needed to put my best foot forward to be successful; these petty temperament issues of my team members could not decide the success of my career moves. I gathered myself and decided to take myself out of the negative influence of such behavior. I kept a positive attitude despite her negative reactions. She would talk to everyone except me. Every morning when I greeted her, she never responded, and seconds later, if anyone else in the team arrived, she would chat with them for a long time. It was so obvious that she had decided to have this negative behavior toward me despite my constant attempts to build a connection. Her impolite behavior continued for months. In one of my discussions with my manager George, I alluded to this ongoing behavior challenge with my team member and how it was impacting me at work. He patiently listened to me and replied, "You cannot win everyone's heart. If a tennis player, while playing a tennis match, focuses on what the crowd, referee, opponent, and other people on the court think of him more than his game, it will impact his performance. Even if there are non-supporters in the crowd, it doesn't imply that he is not at his very best. There are times when impolite comments are hurled at him to distract him; he must continue to focus on his goal to win. Probably, those non-supporters are supporting their opponent or simply love to criticise while they are comfortably seated in their chairs. Let me give you another example to explain the situation to you." he continued.

"Have you noticed when a farmer sows seeds of a crop, it is common to have weeds grow beside them. These weeds are plants that can hamper the growth of actual crops by exhausting them of the required resources. Imagine your career as your own field of valuable crops. Will you let the weed feed the resources that your crops need? In our lives, too, we will meet different sorts of people but be smart enough to identify these weeds, aka negative influences that stunt your growth by feeding on your energy".

This was an important lesson for me to be aware of the negative influence around me and act upon it by distancing myself from them or not dwelling too much on their behaviour. Within 1 year of these encounters, Esha's husband secured a job in a different country, requiring her to move too. During her farewell lunch, when poked by another team member to elaborate on her cold behaviour towards me, she confessed her uncanny behaviour spiralled due to the insecurities that cropped up within her when I joined the team. She explained how she felt unsettled by my experience and the confidence that I exhibited. "I envied you and was concerned that you would take my spot as 'the best' in the team". It was a respite to know because for a long time, I did contemplate, 'What if, I am at fault here or unknowingly I have caused hurt to her.'

Many a time, we relinquish our personality and get lost in the overcast of the negative influences around us. These influences do not appear with a label warning as seen on a pack of cigarettes- "Smoking is injurious to your health" or with some unpleasant pictures depicting the ill effects of Smoking to petrify you. Negative influences are all around us in our families, at work and every nook and corner of the world. The solution to ward off the negative influence is to know them to decide for yourself. We cannot avoid them by not mentioning them or closing our eyes if meet. The beauty is in identifying and acting upon how it can be eliminated from our space, just like the weeds.

I remember when I was leaving for my engineering college in Mumbai and planned to stay alone. My dad warned me, "Stay away from drugs, smoking, alcohol. Always feel free to ask us when in doubt." One simple statement had such an impact on me that I continued to have a strong connection with my family. The first few months in the hostel, I had a nasty roommate who thought she could coax me and use my monthly expenditure money to feed her smoking habits. In fact, I did get under her influence in no time, happily handing over money for her smoking and drinking habits as she made false promises to return it at the earliest. That day never arrived, and when I confronted her, she accused me of making false claims. I felt devastated, as I was adhering to her as an elder sister in a new city to find my ground. Thanks to my family, I could share it with them and was guided to stay strong until I got the opportunity to shift into another room away from her shadows. I continued to live in the same room as her but never responded to her antagonising behavior. I had identified her as a negative influence, and now I could act on removing her from my space.

It could have been catastrophic if I had allowed that behavior to continue. The negative impact of her negative influence could have robbed me of my peace of mind. With a little encouragement and support from my loved ones, I could activate the muscle to identify the negative influence and act upon it. There is a common misconception that only people can be negative influences, although the fact is that our very own habits can be the root of a negative influence or attract more negative influences into our life.

I recall when the world was introduced to content providers like Netflix, Amazon Prime, and others. I was so excited to explore the option of watching regional content or global content from anywhere and anytime. The dinner time for our family slowly turned into binge-watching that continued late into the evenings, past our bedtimes. We, as a family, were losing control of our life and slowly slipping into the web of endless entertainment available at our fingertips. The impact was inevitable; we were waking up tired with the feeling of incomplete sleep and putting on weight as we cherished the sofa more than our running shoes. The monotonous cycle filled with a variety of screens providing entertainment had to break. Gladly, we had identified the negative influence on us as a family and individuals. I took charge of it, and we gradually migrated back to the dining table for dinner without screens. The sleep time was respected, with leeway on the weekends.

Finally, we came out of the unconscious negative influence that we had adhered to; it was hidden as something providing us comfort and entertainment. The negative influences, sometimes disguised as comfort providers, are deeply rooted in our lifestyle or simply emerge from our childhood experiences. In fact, in our rushed lives, we miss pausing to notice that we ourselves are acting as a negative influence for our kids. If we think about it, in our gardens, it is our responsibility to get rid of the weeds to allow the garden to thrive. Whose responsibility will it be to ensure we are removing weeds, aka negative influences, from our own lives or our kids' lives? One mustn't forget that home is a child's first school and parents are their first teachers. Like we learned from our parents, our pets, kids continue to learn from us too.

This should be no surprise that it is the same for the wider animal kingdom too. Numerous research has advocated that children from a very early age get influenced by their parents and people surrounding them in those tender years. These influences can be positive or negative. However, the child is too young to classify these influences as positive or negative. With time, as parents, we play a pivotal role in setting positive examples and equipping them with knowledge to identify these influences. We must develop resiliency to thrive in our disparate environments embedded with various elements.

From my experience of almost four decades, I have created a few questions to qualify someone or something as a negative influence in life.

- Is someone's behaviour making you uncomfortable or causing stress?
- Are you listening to someone's demands to avoid negative behaviour from them?
- What is that you regret about your time after you have lost time doing it for hours, missing your crucial activities?

- Have you noticed anything impacting your health, a habit, a substance or someone's comments or association?
- Do you feel guilty after doing something that you weren't sure to do but were compelled to do by someone?
- Are you constantly expected to act in a certain way and are not accepted the way you are?

An important aspect of living a weed-free life is to develop a skill to identify them. Once you identify that a plant in your garden is a weed, you can ensure measures are taken to prevent them from thriving. For example, in the UK, the Japanese knotweed has been classified as an invasive species. It spreads rapidly, forming dense thickets that crowd and shade out native vegetation. This reduces species diversity, alters natural ecosystems, and negatively impacts wildlife habitat. In fact, if a house or a property hosts Japanese knotweed, the property rates can decline, and the homeowner is legally obliged to control the weed before it spreads further. They are known to cause damage both to the property and the environment.

Because of its invasive nature, it must be removed by an expert because you might try pulling them off the ground, but even if a tiny rhizome is dispersed, it will sprout again. The point being, not all weeds can be controlled by the same solution. Some of them can be merely tackled by spraying a weed controller, but others might be so deep-rooted that they would need expert intervention to be controlled or excluded. It is never too late to identify these weeds not only in your garden but in your life, before they take control of it. Moreover, one must not be shy to take help from experts to remove these devastating negative influences from their life to enjoy the precious gift of life.

Chapter 7
Imperfection is Perfect

"Ma, I don't like how I look now. I used to look good when I was a baby," my 15-year-old nephew Avi commented as he looked at him in a mirror.

"Why do you say so?" my sister asked him inquisitively, a bit worried about his remark.

"Don't know, but my face is different with lots of changes, a bit imperfect!" Avi replied, still looking at himself and touching his face.

"Avi, that's not right! You are not imperfect, you are growing, changing for good. Make this mirror your friend, a reliable friend. What you see in it is reality; it is showing you who you are, showing Avi who is growing." I tried explaining to Avi as my sister groaned and placed her hand on her forehead.

"Aunty, I don't feel good, the change petrifies me. I am confused about where it will lead me," Avi sulked as he turned away to leave the room.

"You are going through a process, Avi. Have you seen a painter paint on the canvas?" I enquired of Avi as he was almost at the door to flee the conversation. Avi paused, walked towards a seat beside my sister, and replied, "Yes, I paint sometimes!" as he got comfortable on the sofa.

"Ok, a painter starts with a single stroke of color combined with varied strokes and colors to paint the picture. If you start judging his painting before he has finished, you will not understand and will feel confused. The half-finished canvas might not be appealing to you as you are unable to look ahead at what is yet to be painted. Avi, nothing is permanent, we can't be kids forever. We all are in the process of making; we are different paintings in different stages of life:

an infant, a toddler, a young kid, tween, teen, young adult, middle-aged, and so on. The picture will evolve with time, and your wisdom will too. Don't judge yourself. It is okay to be imperfect. Don't get overwhelmed by what you see on social media as you do your "Social Media Mindless Scrolling (SMSS)". What you see in the mirror is the real you and not the Avi in a picture frame from 10 years ago or Avi smiling behind a filter in a social media app," I spoke to Avi, hoping a teenager would pay attention to me as I criticised his lifeline social media apps.

Avi nodded and said, "Aunty, I hear you, I look like a handsome man in the making!" and chuckled as he hugged me tight.

Surprisingly, he agreed to what I said and added a few more comments on how what we see behind the screen is not always true. I was delighted to see so much wisdom trickling down from a young adult.

"Great conversation, Avi. If ever you have a doubt about yourself, look into the mirror to accept yourself as you are. Take a moment to appreciate how you have grown with time to be what you are. By the way, your grandma wasn't always as old as she is today. It is a natural aging process that makes us complete." I gave him a pat on his shoulder to cheer him up.

He was led to think he is imperfect as he had been gathering an expectation to look and act perfect. It was important for someone to remind him that 'imperfection is perfect'. It makes me ponder, how did I learn my lesson on embracing imperfection as a crucial element of my self-discovery and growth? Going back in time, it was a couple of years ago, and I was speaking to my mentor at work about how I could upskill myself and take up a new challenge to experiment with my learning skills at the same time.

"Priyanka, if you wish to do exciting learning and stay relevant, you must do research on NLP and its application in Telecoms" my manager said.

While he was talking, I quickly googled NLP to make sense of it.

"It will be nice to get your research documented by next week, as I have a pretty packed schedule for the next 3-4 weeks" My mentor smiled with a glimmer in his eye.

"Perfect, sounds exciting, Thanks!", I walked away smiling on the outside after completing our conversation and bewildered from inside with the thought of research I'll have to do and present it to an intellectual like him.

As the weeks passed, I found myself avoiding the task, paralysed by the fear of producing something imperfect. When my mentor finally asked about my progress, I felt a wave of dread. 'How did your research go?' he messaged. My fingers hovered over the keyboard, but all I could manage was a reluctant 'Ok.' I continued with my usual projects, hoping to delay the inevitable confrontation."

God had some stirring plans for me, I walked up to the coffee machine and there he was with a cup of coffee. I greeted him and began the conversation on different topics, cleverly trying to escape the NLP topic. He was stubborn and probed me again if I had a draft that he could review.

I gave up and responded that I have been struggling and unfortunately my draft is not perfect to be shared.

He started laughing hysterically and replied "A draft is never perfect! We all are drafts and even when your document will be final, it will not be perfect. It will be read by distinct people with diverse points of views and ways of writing, so you literally can never be perfect. So why fret? Go ahead and please share the not so perfect draft with me, I am not a perfectionist".

I was still standing next to the coffee machine with an empty mug in my hand wondering, why did I wait for several weeks to share the document for a review? A funny thought tickled me and made me smile as I lifted my filled coffee mug.

"Do I skip my meal to get home and have a perfect meal with my family? Or when I am taking medication for an ailment, would I avoid going for a follow up until I am perfectly alright? Or I refuse to sit in the office chair because it is not as perfect as the one, I have at my home" I questioned myself as I walked back to my desk, still smiling.

An impromptu conversation at the coffee station was a real eye-opener. I have been delaying my progress by keeping my thoughts, research work to myself. My apprehension to share a draft was excluding the feedback loop from the mentors until I finished it fully. Isn't it pretty much like the software waterfall model, where the software designers take the requirements in the beginning followed by development work, testing, implementation and feedback. However, the business environment these days is so dynamic that there can be changes in the business requirement during the process. There is a high possibility that the product that will be implemented without a feedback loop until it is fully ready might not match the requirements. Hence the Agile ways of working are recommended wherein there is a constant feedback loop mechanism with more flexibility on delivering on the requirements. Basically, I wasn't collaborating with my mentor to validate my understanding of his tasks as I developed a document as a deliverable.

"It makes so much sense," I said loudly, catching the attention of my colleague Rajshree sitting next to me.

"What makes so much sense? Do you care to share?" she prodded with a wide smile and turned away towards her computer screen.

"Raj, I have learnt how important it is to be confident about ourselves, our work and stop idealising a perfect world, home, project, job, child, spouse, pet, and everything that we wish to be perfect. The reality is we all need a little nudge, help to evolve. Our imperfections make space for our strengths and weaknesses to exist together. I have been apprehensive for a long time to share my thoughts as I struggle to find the perfect words or create a perfect work environment. It is a myth as imperfections exist to take monotony from our lives. Sorry for a long sermon but I just received wisdom from my mentor, don't mind me" I sighed as I felt relaxed to know that I have passed on the wisdom and played it back to me to imbibe it completely forever.

"I need a cup of tea now, let's go" Rajshri got up from her seat and hushed me along to the coffee station.

Discussing it further with Rajshri led me to profound thoughts about how imperfect people come together to create a perfect team. I am not great at commercials, but Rajshri is a commercial expert. I do the technical sales; she can price it and similarly others in our team function as a unit to succeed. A cricket team, football team, your team they bring their strengths together to create strong teams. For these teams to be perfect, every single member of the team must work on sharpening their strengths like a chisel and overshadow each other's weaknesses. Like the pieces of jigsaw, all the pieces are not perfect, but they come together to create a perfect picture.

Speaking of the marvel of teamwork, it will be unfair if I don't mention one of the largest and most complex projects that I led. The project required us to build a proposal to meet the customer's requirements, which were more than 4000 lines. Moreover, it needed compliance, proofs, and the cherry on top was the stringent timelines. I had a team of 7 architects allocated to support me as a design lead and ensure we responded with our proposal for this billion-dollar project in approximately 29 days. The whole process entailed taking it through our organisation's internal governance, building solutions with multiple partners and vendors, getting approvals from various stakeholders, plus many other tasks. The crucial bit was documenting the response that would be close to 900 pages after completion.

I was amazed to be part of that team; we all brought different strengths to the table and the synchronicity with which we worked alongside each other to build the response was magnificent. I could visualise us as a pack of crayons, wherein every colour has its own effect and together we could create a beautiful picture. Had I been alone on the task in hand, I would have struggled to get everything in order and bring out the effect that others did with their contribution. Just like the colours, they are perfect in colouring in their shades or their strengths and are not designed to colour as other colours too. Yet they are perfect in where their strength lies.

Even in our personal lives, we keep looking for the perfect partner, perfect relationships, and everything perfect. The word 'prefect' is quite a stout word that sets an expectation of all the desired qualities, attributes to be present in the subject up for dialogue. It is great to dream of a perfect everything, the glistening truth is that we all have imperfections that make us perfect in different environments and settings. These flaws adorn us as much as our strengths. We've to accept each other's flaws and appreciate our strengths. In my home, I am the talkative, impatient and the hot-headed one and my spouse is equally calm, easy-going, and has good listening skills. Instead of dwelling on our weaknesses or assassinating our characters to our penchants, we have accepted each other as a whole package to mold a relationship that grows with each passing day. We both have strived for excellence rather than being a perfect couple; excellence in being always there for each other.

To emphasise on the point of acquiring perfection with time and when we begin imperfection is natural, I have a story to share. I read this post on the Internet, where a man narrated the story that his teacher shared with his class. A pottery teacher split her class into two halves to explain the value of the process that takes you to perfection. To get to perfection you must go through numerous iterations to extract the perfect.

To the first half the teacher said, "You will spend the semester studying pottery, planning, designing, and creating your perfect pot. At the end of the semester, there will be a competition to see whose pot is the best".

To the other half she said, "You will spend your semester making lots of pots. Your grade will be based on the number of completed pots you finish. At the end of the semester, you'll also have the opportunity to enter your best pot into a competition."

The first half of the class threw themselves into their research, planning, and design. Then they set about creating their one, perfect pot for the competition.

The second half of the class immediately grabbed fistfuls of clay and started churning out pots. They made big ones, small ones, simple ones, and intricate ones. Their muscles ached for weeks as they gained the strength needed to throw so many pots.

At the end of class, both halves were invited to enter their most perfect pot into the competition. Once the votes were counted, all the best pots came from the students that were tasked with quantity. The practice they gained made them significantly better potters than the planners on a quest for a single, perfect pot. In life, the best way to be perfect and immaculate while learning a skill, is to make a lot of pots.

Perfection is excellence in what we do. It is developed over time with the progress made each single day. A continuous process that persists throughout your lifetime to achieve this impeccability in various things we do.

It is aspirational to strive for perfection, but imperfection must not become an impediment in the path of our progress.

- Take out some time to focus on the outcomes more than the aesthetics.
- Sometimes, it is better not to take too long to deliver a perfect outcome but keep progressing the requirements by showing the drafts that you have developed.
- We all are drafts and are being perfected every single day as we live our lives.
- Appreciate the journey that one takes to get to excellence.

Let me leave you with a thought to ponder over, imperfection leads us to perfection. That's why it is crucial to embrace imperfection at every level to get better as we observe, experience and learn. Why don't you take a pause, reflect and take a note of what are the different aspects of your lives that are unexplored as you continuously judge yourself? It will be a good start to make a list of projects, ideas, and aspirations that were left in the backburner for quite a sometime, as you waited for them to be a perfect plan. Now is your moment to plan that holiday, a date, the course you wanted to take, the house you wanted to buy, or a start-up you wanted to set-up. Roll-up your sleeves, conquer your fears, befriend mistakes to learn as you embark on this journey to continue to evolve. Let's talk more about how to befriend and learn from your mistakes in the next chapter.

Chapter 8

Mistake? Learn and Retake!

Have you ever experienced that surge of invincibility when you feel so empowered that lifting mountains seems within your reach? Almost a decade ago, I felt exactly like that when I started working in a customer-facing role. The passion for understanding customer requirements and designing as per their desired outcomes was ruling my head. I was new in my role in this organisation with many enterprise customers. My job required frequent travel for business meetings within different cities in India. Having several accounts meant various customers across the country and working with a set of people internally.

As the pressure was mounting with the demand to travel with account managers to various meetings, conflicting schedules became a new normal. In this very situation, Manya and Dinesh both booked my calendar for back-to-back trips. I agreed to travel from Mumbai to Bangalore with Manya on the 10th of July, returning to Mumbai the same night and flying to Udaipur the next morning with Dinesh for another executive-level meeting. I was comfortable with the idea and started my preparations for both meetings in disparate parts of the country.

On the day I arrived in Bangalore after leaving Mumbai around 7 AM with Manya, I had a successful day. We were back in Mumbai the same evening, and by the time I stepped into my home, it was 10 PM. I had time left for a meagre 4-hour sleep before I had to get ready and leave for the airport again to meet my other commitment to be in Udaipur. We had set an alarm for 3 AM to get ready to board the flight at 6:30 AM. I entrusted the alarms and the sound of alarms to be loud enough to wake us.

"What's the time?" I enquired in sleep as I tossed to the edge of the bed.

"What!!!" I jumped out of bed as I looked at my phone showing 5 AM with my squinted eyes.

With my face flushed and feeling giddy, I hurriedly shook Pritam, my spouse, to wake up.

We both rushed to the airport with me still checking for my belongings in my handbag and changing out of my night suit in the car. I arrived at the airport to find I had missed boarding the flight by 4 minutes. It was so stressful as my colleague Dinesh was trying to convince the airline staff while I was on my way to allow me as it was important for me to be there for the meeting in Udaipur.

"What are my options?" I asked the airline staff as I was desperate to get to Udaipur.

"You can take the next flight to Jaipur in 45 minutes and go to Udaipur by Road from there", she explained very confidently.

I instantly decided to continue with a new plan. I bought a ticket to Jaipur and boarded the next flight while my colleague was in mid-air on her flight to Udaipur. As I was sitting on that not-so-busy flight, a nosy middle-aged man sitting on the other side of the almost vacant flight enquired.

"So, what is taking you to Jaipur" he seemed interested to know, why a bemused girl still partially half asleep, is travelling to Jaipur in the early morning hours.

"Oh, I have a meeting in Udaipur today, I missed my flight. I plan to get there by 1PM" I replied to him without expecting the next statement would wake me up.

"You will take at least 7 hours by car to get to Udaipur" he explained and seemed a bit taken aback with my travel plans and probably judged my planning skills.

This was the moment, I felt my heart sinking, ears numbing and shock spreading throughout my body. I decided to stay quiet after this revelation. I thanked him for this crucial piece of information that wasn't given to me when

I was desperately looking for a solution to get into Udaipur at the earliest, after missing my original flight. I couldn't think of anything else now, only how I have failed in fulfilling my desire to be super productive and available. I have failed to please everyone and prioritise myself before committing to the trip. The rest of the flight time was spent with closed eyes, imagining the reaction from Manish, my manager and how I had made a fool of myself.

We arrived at Jaipur, and during those days, there weren't many flight options for non-metro cities. I still had a random thought of checking if there was a flight to Udaipur from Jaipur. My every move to make myself present at this meeting was going against me. I could see it clearly by now that a mistake, a BIG MISTAKE, had happened. I made another mistake to correct one mistake, and I needed to stop now. I called up my manager and informed him of the difficult situation I had created for myself. He assured me that he would speak to our senior executive to get an exemption for me and advised me to return. The next call was to my husband to arrange for a flight back to Mumbai, as I didn't intend to make any further decisions for the day. I had to pause and reflect. As I waited for my flight ticket, I saw a sweet shop with my favorite traditional delicacy—"Ghewar." I decided if I had come so far, why should I go home empty-handed?

Believe me, it was the most expensive sweet I have ever had. Thanks to my manager Manish, he got an exemption for the Mumbai-Udaipur, Mumbai-Jaipur journey. Neither was it debited from my payout nor was I penalised. However, I was warned to be extra cautious in the future while planning my meetings. The mistake I made early in my career was a great lesson for me. Hats off to my employer, who decided to give me another chance to learn from it rather than penalising me.

Making a mistake didn't mean that I would not go to customer meetings anymore or that I was not worthy of going to these meetings. It was a call for me to not overdo myself and to plan my meetings properly. Trust me, I have taken my lesson seriously. I am much more organised, vocal about my limitations to travel, and very punctual when it comes to getting to the airport. Our mistakes teach us a lesson; we must learn from them, be aware, self-analyse, ask for feedback, and have a plan to avoid similar mistakes in the future. "You are more than your mistakes. Be corrigible," my driving instructor, Teresa, told me once. "You make as many mistakes as you want in today's lesson; just don't repeat them." The most important aspect to remember is to learn and reattempt once you have made a mistake.

Some of the mistakes feel incorrigible as if the world ends with them. I am certain there will be mistakes that, if once made, will not give you another opportunity to re-take. Our emphasis here is on situations wherein we have the power to give it another shot. Many a time, a mistake is defined as an action, and the consequence of a mistake can be a failure. What we forget is that mistakes prepare us for the future as we learn our ways around them. A simple mistake cannot take away the essence of 'You'. Remember, 'You' are bigger than your mistakes; they cannot define you! These mistakes contribute indirectly to your success, as they compel you to get better at whatever you wish to do. A mindset change is often required to use these mistakes as a perfect launch pad to learn and retake your desired outcome.

There are different ways to learn from mistakes—our own mistakes, others' mistakes—and that's the reason it is interesting to investigate the past to understand the approach taken by various leaders and, consequently, what they achieved—success or failure. Our own mistakes, right from the early school days, our exam papers when returned, would highlight the mistakes. Our teachers ensured that they shared the answers to all the questions so that we could understand our mistakes to correct them. I recall going over the answers to the exam paper, surprised many times by how I missed answering a simple question or misunderstood it.

Eventually, we do learn to resolve the mistakes by identifying and analysing where we went wrong. I have made many mistakes in my life, and most importantly, I made efforts to correct them. I made mistakes in knowing people's true character and responding to situations in life. Mistakes were made at every step when I learned something new—be it twirling a hula-hoop, swimming, driving, being a mother, or in relationships. We must visualise these mistakes as speed-breakers on the road that slow us down but don't stop us from moving forward. It is important not to be hard on yourself, smile if you make a mistake, take note of what you missed to commit a mistake, and act wisely to take control of those mistakes before they lead you to failure. The mindset that can adapt to these situations is an agile growth mindset. Be that force of persistence, and every time you fall, stand up on your feet and march ahead.

The other day, while scrolling YouTube shorts, I came across the story of a painter who placed his painting in the middle of high street with a note- "If you find a mistake, circle it"

When he returned in the evening to collect his painting, it was filled with 100's of marks that encircled his mistakes. He returned home disappointed and shared it with his mother. The painter's mother was experienced who suggested that this time, her son must put a different note:

"If you find a mistake, correct it"

To the boy's surprise, there were no circles on the drawing. No one cared to correct the mistakes whereas everyone was eager to circle his mistakes. The important lesson being- It is easy to point out mistakes but difficult to correct them. So, it brings a great point across that if you point at a mistake, suggest a way to correct it to allow others to retake it.

As I absorbed the lesson from the painter's experience, I couldn't help but reflect on how often we, too, face a sea of circled errors without guidance on how to correct them. It underscores a wider truth about our approach to mistakes — not as opportunities to learn but as flaws to defend against. Mistakes are often perceived as negative, and individuals are deterred from making a mistake. This may develop a defensive behaviour that inhibits one from learning from their mistake. Instead of learning, adding to their experience, all their energy is invested in defending it.

Inadvertently, as I flipped the page of the quote calendar on my desk, the quote of the day was: "Experience is the name everyone gives to their mistakes." — Oscar Wilde. So true, if one accepts the mistakes and failures to take cue from them to carve out their future endeavours, a growth mindset will prevail. Science has proven allowing the human brain to work freely without the fear of making a mistake fosters innovation. I don't have to go far to find an example to elaborate on it. As a mother, I developed a tendency to interrupt my daughter to expect that she does everything as I do. If she deviated, it flustered me to a great level.

One remark from her, "Mom, I would like to use my own brain, if you allow!" stopped me from incessantly explaining to her the next steps. I realised how my overprotective behavior of being too cautious, listing all the risks, and detailing steps even before she tried her hand at something new like skateboarding, sewing, or simply making a cup of tea for me was limiting her capability. I was afraid to allow her to make a mistake and, in the process, blocked her from developing her own judgment. To my surprise, the whole equation changed between my daughter and me. All this while, I thought she must learn from me to be able to do things properly. However, as I allowed her to take charge of many of these activities, she showed me amazingly new ways of being creative, effective, or simply different. For example, I never thought of crocheting a rabbit with my limited skills in crochet, whereas she managed to learn it through YouTube videos. The result was a beautiful pink crochet stuffed rabbit as my birthday present, all done by herself without any steer from me. We discussed how she managed to succeed in something so complicated.

"Ah, I made many mistakes when I started working on this project, Rabbit. I had to restart a few times to be comfortable with the crochet needle. My other challenge was finding cotton to stuff it. I quickly crocheted a few round balls to use instead of cotton filling. It was alright, I enjoyed it," Tanishka replied, as she explained her experience with crocheting a stuffed toy animal for the first time ever. To my disbelief, I was not only holding her back from experiencing new adventures, but I was losing out on these opportunities to learn from her. The mistakes she made during the process made her perfect as she didn't give up. This is where we allow our minds and knowledge bank to grow. This is one example; our lives offer us various opportunities to look back, learn, and proceed with new knowledge. The onus lies on us to be brave enough to clinch these opportunities without fearing the mistakes that we might make. If mistakes are made, we need to be brave enough to acknowledge and resolve them. Mistake, learn, and retake!

Speaking of being brave, at a very crucial point and with a key client in my career, I made the mistake of sharing the wrong figures for the commitment on performance to our client. As soon as I realised, I ensured it was shared with my key stakeholders—within my organisation and in my client's organisation. I explained the error, acknowledged my mistake, and rectified it with an explanation of the new figures. My client accepted it, as it was clear to them too that the figures I shared were practically impossible. Thanks to my understanding of management and client, I was given an opportunity to explain and resolve. This was my opportunity to learn—not to burn myself—and ensure the documents are peer-reviewed by a fresh pair of eyes before they are shared. I was fortunate that my employer and client gave me an opportunity to resolve. We may not always get an opportunity to retake, even though there will be a lot of learning to prepare us for a new, rejuvenated launch. Let me sum it up for you: how mistakes can be turned around to succeed rather than lead to a failed launch.

Once again, I don't wish to limit your method of learning and cultivating a culture where mistakes are acceptable, and one can learn from them to take another go. However, I have taken the liberty to share a few tips that worked for me to change my mindset:

- Mistakes are not to be feared but an opportunity to learn how we can do things differently with varied outcomes.
- We all make mistakes; the real courage is in accepting our mistakes to learn and plan for a re-take to be successful.
- Repeating the same mistake numerous times might be a call to introspect if you are ready for it or if it is really your strength or weakness. I recall during my college days, I started learning Java, a programming language, and I was consistent in making mistakes wherein I had to switch between upper and lower case. After a while, I identified the reason for my challenge and worked on it specifically to get over the cycle of repetitive mistakes. I did realise programming wasn't my sweet spot, although I completed the course required as part of my curriculum.
- It is perfectly fine to take help from peers, family, and colleagues and not be afraid that they might point out your mistakes. We must be receptive to feedback. In fact, early feedback, like my encounter with a mentor on

producing a paper, is crucial. I waited too long while I strived to find the right way to present it back to him, fearing that it may not be perfect. It is okay to make mistakes but critical to learn from them.

- When you make a mistake, don't just focus on the mistake and be hard on yourself. Look back at the efforts you made to get to where you are. Mistakes can be a stumbling block but not the end of the world.

- When your mistakes make you feel low, think about the massive efforts that our space scientists made to launch a satellite into space. Everything is a work of precision, calculations, and is dependent on a lot of external factors. What you might perceive as a mistake can be a result of various external factors. Look for those signs before you take the blame and sulk into regret.

'To err is human, to forgive is divine' - Let us develop a growth mindset that allows us to freely learn, explore, innovate, and, if mistakes are made, we stand up to them. We all are flawed in one way or another; impeccability is a myth. No wonder it is essential for us to learn to forgive and not bear the burden of being a victim of committing a mistake or being affected by someone's mistake. We all deserve chances to retake after a mistake; after all, we are here to continuously unlearn and learn to stay relevant.

Chapter 9
Love Yourself: You Are Your First Customer

Can an empty pitcher of water quench anyone's thirst? Have you ever heard the story of a traveller named Empty, who was on his journey to find love? He travelled through tough terrains across mountains, swam through the seas and oceans. It was over two years that he was on this arduous journey. He met various people and creatures who helped him to get to his next milestone, Empty felt no gratitude and didn't care to thank them. All he aspired to was to find love and complete his journey. The aspiration to find love was so strong that he forgot to take care of himself.

Days passed and he continued to ignore the pain in his body and one day while he was traversing through a desert, he collapsed in the middle of the desert. As he lay helpless without any food and water, he was noticed by a passing by camel tradesman. He quickly fetched his water bag and offered it to Empty. Unfortunately, there was just one last sip of water left in it for Empty to drink. The tradesman carried empty on his camel's back to his house. The loving family of the tradesman ensured that Empty was given the right care. When he gathered his strength, he thanked the tradesman and his family. He questioned the tradesman-

"Why did you help me and not let me die there?" Empty had a confused look on his face as he had nothing left to give to the tradesman for his kindness.

"Empty, I did what I would have wished for anyone else to do with me, If I were in the same situation. You cannot expect goodness without being kind like you cannot find love until you learn to love. You ought to give to be able to receive. Can I quench your thirst from an empty water bag? I need to fill it up with water to be able to drink water from it. Fill yourself with love my friend and you will find love wherever you live." The tradesman smiled; hugged him and prepared his camel to give him a ride to his next destination.

Empty parted with this emptiness inside him that compelled him to travel distant lands and tread on an onerous journey. It made him reflect on the journey that he had been on for the last two years and how he missed opportunities to be kind, grateful and love back.

Empty is no stranger and sometimes lives inside all of us wherein we are so driven about our ambitions and aspirations that we forget to love ourselves, others and appreciate our very existence. As a starter, self-love is not easy, we measure ourselves against tough baselines; we then rate ourselves as lacking against these measures. Yes, this is the point where a villain enters- negative feelings. Unconsciously, we continue to spread this negativity in our day-to-day interactions.

I remember as the youngest child; sibling of 3 beautiful sisters and being around them, I developed lots of inferiority complexes. I was nine years old and worried that I am not as tall as them. Essentially, they were my yardstick to measure my physical appearance. It wasn't great for me as there was no chance that I could meet the standards of a 17, 21 and a 22-year-old young girl. Silently, it was affecting me as I was concerned about my future! Gosh, what a worrisome child I was. Thankfully my sister was sharp enough to spot that I wasn't being myself.

"Pichu, why are you so upset? What shall we do to make you smile?" Anjali, my sister asked me as she caressed my hair. It didn't take me long to melt by her love and open my heart.

"You all are so tall, beautiful and everyone loves talking to you. I am short, ugly and no one wants me. Even mom and dad love you more." I snivelled with tears rolling out of my eyes.

"Who told you this? My dearest little sister, have you ever seen your eyes, they are so big and beautiful. I love the curls and bounce in your hair, wish I had hair like you. Regarding your height, you are yet to grow. Are you doing the stretches that I taught you a few months ago?" She replied, assuring me.

I nodded for the stretches while my brain was grappling with the new information that was shared with me about my eyes, hair and potential to grow. It made me so comfortable in my own skin and raised my self-love. I remember how I spent time in front of the mirror appreciating my eyes. A little talk helped me raise myself in my own eyes and spread love.

We all need that someone in our life to make us realise that we are valuable, beautiful inside out. If you ever find someone who needs that nudge to love themselves, don't be afraid to gently appreciate them on their strengths. We all have our unique strengths that we can be proud of and be a little self-appreciative.

Through the journey of self-discovery and learning to cherish ourselves, we pave the way to understanding our true worth—both internally and externally. Just as we must fill our own reservoirs of love to truly connect with and love others, we must also believe in our own value to effectively offer our talents to the world. This realisation leads us to an important shift in perspective: seeing ourselves as our first and most important customer. If we don't buy into our own worth, how can we expect others to see the value in what we provide?" Have you ever thought about who your first customer is?

It was a summer fair in my school. I had to run a food stall with my own food item. All the sale would go to a charity; the individual with the highest sale will be given a special prize and a certificate. I came home super excited to share my idea with my family. I wanted to sell vegetable noodles made by my dad, my favourite food those days.

"I need to get all the ingredients for the Vegetable noodles, so that papa can prepare at least 20 portions for me to sell in the summer fair." I explained it with urgency as summer fair was just a week away.

"Vegetable noodles? No, let's do something simpler. It will save time in the morning, and you can manage it in school. I suggest let's do potato dumplings" Mum responded to my excited ask as I sulked with her response.

It was the morning of summer fair; all the preparations were done in the school for me to set-up my stall. I arranged my stall and displayed the name "Potato Dumplings' ' on a white board with a red marker. As I stood there, my eyes were busy looking at other food stalls with a discontentment that I don't have the best food item.

"I could have won, if I had "Vegetable Noodles" in my stall." I repeated this thought to myself numerous times.

I sold only 5 Potato dumplings that day and certainly couldn't beat the "Aloo Tikki", the winning food stall with the highest earnings.

As I was busy packing my items from the food stall, group of teachers passing by tasted the Potato dumpling and were absolutely amazed by the flavours. I ended up finishing all the potato dumplings as the word spread about the crispy, well-done food I was serving.

This episode made me think, if I could sell all the 25 dumplings in a matter of minutes, why didn't I sell them all?

I failed to believe in my own product that made it challenging to sell it to others. If I didn't have an intention to buy my own product as I didn't believe it to be the best or ignored it to understand what makes it unique, how could I possibly sell it to my customers? You are your first customer as I was my first customer, who didn't expect any flavours from a rather simple potato dumpling.

Remarkably, we miss the guileless power of understanding what we possess, eventually dwindling to believe in our competencies. You can only be what you believe you are. Many a time in life we fail to climb a mountain as we don't believe in our potential to climb it. Self- belief is a fuel that can fire us up to do things that we were made to believe were impossible. A different perspective to a challenge offers us opportunities to grow and explore our true potential; a potential that's hidden from the world. There is a popular story I read on the internet of three candidates applying for a job as a salesman. The Interviewer tasks the aspiring Salesmen with the task of selling combs to monks. The most successful salesman out of these three stood out because of his knowledge, intent and belief in the product he was selling. So, what exactly happens in this story?

The first salesman manages to sell a comb to one monk with the idea that he could use it for scratching his itchy scalp. The second one sold around ten by suggesting to a monk that his visitors had very messy hair due to the strong winds they faced while walking to the temple.

He convinced the monk to give out combs to the visitors so they could tidy themselves up and show greater respect during their worship. The successful third salesman sold 1000 combs as he had a great plan, he proposed to the senior master of the monks that they can gift a comb engraved with their message to their worshippers as a memento. A comb is an everyday item, as they will use it every day it is likely that they will read the message and feel gratitude. What a thought! To be able to think like that, he must have first believed in the idea of selling followed by knowing what a comb can be sold for in unusual situations like these where his customer base is different and finally his belief that he can plan it out to make it possible.

It all ties back to your self-belief in your skills and capabilities. One must believe in oneself to be able to radiate confidence required to succeed. There have been so many success stories in different parts of the world- A successful discovery by a scientist or a great empire built by an industrialist, self-belief seems to be a common ingredient. I can't stop myself from mentioning the success Nelson Mandela achieved in his fight against apartheid; he had the power to unite people to come together for a common purpose. He believed in his leadership qualities and took the role that was much required in the society in that period.

Great philanthropist and industrialist, Ratan Naval Tata, won people's hearts across the globe for his efforts in supporting social causes that mattered, be it finding a cure for cancer or building kennels for stray dogs. He aspired to make the dream of owning a car true for every Indian. The 'Nano' launched by Tata wasn't a great success but allowed millions of people to believe in their capability to buy and own a car. What drove him to aspire, invest, and contribute to society? He was led by his self-belief that he had the power to drive change or achieve the impossible. Once we get used to the idea of self-belief or accepting our capability to achieve what we want or what no one ever dreamt of, we can carve our way. As the famous saying goes, "Where there is a will, there is a way." It is a mantra that can be applied to any aspect of your life, be it your career progression or personal, professional relationships that you build throughout your life. They are a clear result of what you think of yourself.

If you think you do not belong in a boardroom, that door will never open for you. If you are confident that one day you will be in that boardroom, today will be your day one, as we discussed in the previous chapters. All these journeys begin with a simple acknowledgment and belief in our own capabilities. Would you buy the idea of you sitting in that boardroom or appearing on a TV show or in a meeting with your idol? Be your first customer, then sell the dream that you want, and you will get the results.

Sometimes, we discount ourselves as suitable for a certain meeting or an occasion even before we can secure an opportunity. The reason is simple: we have a very cruel lens which we use to scrutinise ourselves. Looking through this lens, it is natural for us to imagine that the world sees us exactly the way we see ourselves, which isn't true. We are so conscious that every person who catches our eye or is looking at us would make us nervous about our choice of clothes, looks, etc. At this moment, we must remind ourselves of our ability to be sufficient as we are at that moment to confidently go about our daily jobs. If you don't trust your proficiencies, you will be voiding yourself of a successful career, no matter how good you are.

Even when you are planning to apply for jobs and prepare for interviews, you must sell your candidature to yourself. You cannot be successful in an interview process if you don't believe you deserve the job. The first step is to let yourself know that you are the right person for the role. Gradually, as the interview process draws closer, you can sell your candidature to your interviewers. Here, I would like to draw your attention to your self-discovery process. Identify who you are. What are your strengths, weaknesses; what defines you as a person? Appreciate the goodness within you, allow it to grow to do more. Be ready to allude to your aspirations and destination. If you develop clarity to see yourself as a success, you will be able to succeed in whatever you may wish to do. If Steve Jobs never believed in his product, he wouldn't have founded a great company like Apple. One must first be in harmony with their dreams to be able to sell dreams to others.

I have a simple exercise for you to develop a strong feeling of loving yourself and you being the first customer.

- Think of your strengths and situations where you have put them to use for good. Be appreciative of your strengths and feel the love you deserve.
- Have a conversation with different people in your circle and ask for their feedback on what you bring to the team, family of your relationships. It will help you realise why you are loved by others and why you must continue loving yourself.
- Create your self-affirmation to remind yourself of your goodness and practise it in front of a mirror or record to listen to it anytime you doubt yourself. I gave an affirmation written on a piece of paper to my mother to help her post her retirement, as she struggled in her new life as a retiree.
- Next time you prepare food, don't eat it and let others share feedback of how it tastes. It will be impossible for you to accept feedback without getting a taste of it. Right? You must love it first before you can share it with others.
- Try selling a painting for $100 that you bought for $5 from a high-street store. You will never be convinced that it can fetch that much amount. Now imagine if a famous tennis player or a football player signs it for you. Can you still do that?
- Draw a tree with its roots being your core foundational values and the branches of what you believe your strengths are; repeat it but this time add your weaknesses too. When did you feel stronger? Do you know what are your strengths to play on and believe in you?

As we journey through life, embracing who we are and how we fit into this world, it becomes clear that our path is less about reaching a destination and more about growing a little each day. Oscar Wilde once said, 'To love oneself is the beginning of a lifelong romance.' This reminds us that when we fully embrace ourselves, we gain the confidence to show our real selves to others, ensuring that what we offer is accepted and truly appreciated. Remember, the most important commitment we can make is to ourselves.

Section 2
Building Positive Habits

Once we have mastered the art of connecting with ourselves and start learning from our mistakes, why not build some positive habits that help us cement these learnings further? In this section, we will discover simple yet powerful daily habits to enforce the value of self, respecting others and being grateful for what we possess. Having said that, we will touchdown on the other key aspects of inculcating financial habits alongside the habits that develop a stronger you. Next time you will not be in a rush to prepare for your annual review but will have a well-developed personal development plan, if you manage to adapt on your own accord.

"Your beliefs become your thoughts,

Your thoughts become your words,

Your words become your actions,

Your actions become your habits,

Your habits become your values,

Your values become your destiny."

– Gandhi

Chapter 10
Believe in Gratitude

It was early evening as I sat quietly in the garden, writing in my gratitude journal. Tanishka came looking for me and exclaimed

"Mom, I've been looking for you all around the house and here you are in the garden. What are you writing? Is it important?" She questioned as she placed both her hands on her waist dropping her weight on one leg, still trying to figure out what I am writing.

"Yes, it is important that I express gratitude for all the goodness in my life, including you." I replied as I hastened to write another sentence in my journal.

"Leave it and let's go inside please, mom. I want you to help me in setting up my new tablet" she encouraged me to accompany her.

"Ok, I will; You answer one question before we go, what are you grateful for?" I probed her as she held my hand to take me inside and I gathered my things.

"Family, Food, Friends and Phone" She giggled and ran back into the house.

It transported me back to the time when my daughter was three. The busy schedules, travelling to and from work, taking care of my daughter and myself was time-consuming. I realised that for quite some time I hadn't travelled outside of India while my spouse was travelling for business to various countries across Asia Pacific. I was getting snappy, tired and shattered or I was feeling negative about my whole life. One day my sister Shikha called up and was super excited to share about the book she read, Secret by Rhonda Byrne. She couldn't stop singing praises about how it is so simple to read and was convinced that I will enjoy it. Now I was on a mission, we didn't have Amazon next delivery back then, so I managed to buy it from a bookstore while coming home from work. I must say, this is exactly what I needed at that point. I enjoyed reading as I flipped through pages quickly to know more. I arrived home, happy with a grin on my face, as if I had discovered answers to my discontentment. The quest to uncover more was increasing, so I managed to read the other two books- The Magic and The Power too voraciously. I now had the power of the universe at my disposal to achieve my dreams. I had to be conscious of what I have and express gratitude for it.

After a few days, I had a note stuck inside my cupboard that had three things I had set my intention on; ready to surrender to the power of the universe to make it happen.

- Thanks for an international trip sponsored by my organisation.
- Thanks for a fun trip abroad with friends and family.
- Thanks for my daughter's admission in our desired school.

I did go on a fun-trip with my sister to Singapore and had a great time meeting my friends living there. In another year, I went back to Singapore on a business trip that was highly unlikely for anyone from the organisation to travel to. Yes, I managed to secure admission for my daughter in our desired school. What was this? I was unconsciously working towards my goals; the power of the universe was conspiring to make it happen for me. That's the power of practising gratitude, once we make it a point to develop positive feelings towards our goals, unaware we are making way for it.

I haven't stopped practising gratitude till date and carry a gratitude journal with me on my holidays too. It has become such a calming and meditative experience for me to simply thank for our existence and the most overlooked resources - Food, water, air, space, clothing, family, love, job, appreciation for all, kindness and a beautiful life. As I count my blessings every day for a few minutes, it gives me courage to fight for more, for them and for me. By giving your 5 minutes to practice gratitude develops a different mindset within you, a mindset that wouldn't complain if it rains or there is a queue. The restlessness, the desire to have everything perfect transforms into acceptance, admiration and aspiration founded on positive feelings.

As Rhonda Byrne says in her book- The Power" Whatever you are grateful for multiplies. Gratitude is the great multiplier." I have truly witnessed the gratitude multiply my positive emotions as I consistently thanked with a positive attitude. This knowledge empowered me to believe to achieve rather than achieve to believe. The positive belief in my capabilities motivated me to achieve it with the confidence that anything is possible. I could see it happening as I aligned my actions with my belief. Not only the positive attitude multiplied, I flourished personally and professionally. I expressed gratitude to the universe; my almighty for my good health, the ability to think and aspire, a loving family that supports me. I realised soon that the world has everything, it is on us what we are looking for. If the aspiration, admiration is for goodness, it will follow you. I experience gratitude as the tool that could lead me to my goals and carve an enjoyable path. All I had to do was to begin with a small change. An attitude of gratitude, by living and breathing it.

To connect with it I started by practising gratitude in a gratitude journal or simply started thanking the universe for the small achievements and luxuries of life. I could feel myself as worthy of more than I ever imagined before I was introduced to gratitude. The process became so meditative for me as I could see the results; it's a ritual for me. Every day before I go to bed, I take a moment to express my gratitude for the power to get through the day, for the guidance to do the good, the kindness, the good values we thought to our kids and all the pleasures of life. You can build your own gratitude lines or simply start by:

- Saying Thank you for everything aloud when you are clouded by negative thoughts or need that motivation to keep going.
- Purchase a gratitude journal, wherein you can master the art of practising gratitude.
- Inculcate a practice for yourself and your family to share what they are thankful for as you enjoy having a conversation with them and develop a bond.

I started with baby steps; It was difficult to take out time for practising gratitude. It seemed so unworthy of my 5 minutes until I could experience the change. To believe in gratitude it requires a change in attitude. If we start small and thank mother nature for the beautiful blooms, animals, plants that we see around us; we have started right. We can take it further by expressing gratitude for our good health, wealth, prosperity or whatever brings contentment to your mind. Like one must believe in his medication, practitioner before it shows its effects. Gratitude works in a similar way, believe it to experience the power of it. What will you express gratitude for? While you do that remember that's not all. Gratitude is the road that leads to kindness. One of my favourite all-time quotes is "We should certainly count our blessings, but we should also make our blessings count"- Neal A Maxwell. In the next chapter we will explore how developing Kindness and spreading it brings about more abundance and joy. Unfortunately, there are times wherein we forget to be kind as we continue to live our busy lives feeding our families. We will discover how kindness is not a choice but a virtue that one must develop to flourish.

Chapter 11
Never Forget Kindness

The other day I was on a train to get to work, I noticed a young woman sitting right across wearing a badge on her coat. The badge read 'Baby on board". I smiled, what a brilliant idea to ensure others are mindful of a young life you are nurturing within you. As I recall, during my pregnancy days, I have had a few amusing encounters. Almost a decade ago, I was travelling back after a long day at work, and I felt a bit peaky while on the bus. It was a 35-minute-long ride to my home, and I had just got on the bus.

I unquestionably wanted to sit down; nonetheless, I was so conscious and embarrassed to speak out loud that "Excuse me, I need a seat to sit down, can I please take your seat?". Amusingly, even after rallying courage to ask a gentleman, he looked at me in awe and replied, "I am sorry, I have paid for it." and he looked away. I was missing the badge that announced I am pregnant. However, there was a benevolent lady few seats away and she offered me her seat stating she will get down shortly. I continue to remember the lady I met on the bus; I am utterly thankful to her for her kindness when I needed it the most.

During that ride back home, I found myself wondering if we must always announce that we are expecting kind behaviour from people around us, or can we all inculcate kindness in our demeanour? I admire the fact that we are getting braver and share our vulnerabilities with our family, friends, and peers. Although it is impossible to let everyone know what emotions you are always going through. We don't have to be unwell or special to receive kindness in return. It is a trait that must be for all to receive and disseminate. Good news is, Kindness is free and not available in stores to purchase. All you must do is smile, open your heart, and appreciate the differences we bring in our thoughts, appearances, and overall culture.

As a kid, I overheard my mom's conversation with her vivacious friend, Mrs. Arora. She was expressing to her, "You and I, we both are living a good life. A life filled with our responsibilities of raising kids and looking after our families. What I am missing is contributing back to society. There are so many people out there who need help to lead a good life. I wish I could be like you and manage time to involve myself in such activities. It is not easy raising four girls and a full-time job as a schoolteacher".

Mrs. Arora was an easy-going and benevolent lady. She was a schoolteacher like my mother, had 3 children, 2 rabbits and provided lessons to under-privileged children in the evening on different subjects. In addition to that she was a patron of a local blind school for children, where she volunteered every weekend. In addition to all this, she managed to remember everyone's birthdays, get them gifts and be the first one to raise her hand if someone asked for help.

She fittingly replied "Mrs. Mehndiratta, I understand what you mean. Take my advice, make one point to do a kind deed every day. A deed that is not your chore. This will be a great start to give you the courage for more. Why don't you start feeding the birds and then pass on this responsibility to your kids, so that kindness will be multiplied."

My mother was content with her answer and you're right we started feeding the birds the very next day and I learnt to be kind with every passing day. It turned into a daily routine for us to feed the birds; stocking the bird feeders and quietly watching the birds throng to the feed as they filled their bellies with contentment. In a matter of a few days, I could identify the different types of birds that visited us all around the year. A connection was developed between birds and me; even today I start my day by feeding the birds to watch them flutter, interact and chirp with delight.

A passing comment from my mother to inculcate kindness in my everyday life opened my eyes to numerous ways to achieve it. As I worked on developing my Kindness quotient, I did realise that Kindness is an important people skill too. If you aspire to be a great people leader, kindness must be at the core of what you do. Being kind is sometimes misunderstood as being forbearing. At work, it is an expression of emotions that you care for them besides the usual professional engagement, timelines, and deadlines. At some time in my career, I was working on a sales opportunity and was seeking some guidance from one of our technical experts, Matt. Unknowingly, I messaged him to get some time to get answers to my burning questions on the topic. He immediately responded stating his daughter is hospitalised and he will be away for a few days. I managed to get my answers from another expert in the team however, I made it a point to message Matt to check how his daughter is and wished her a speedy recovery.

After a couple of days, Matt resumed work, he contacted me to check if I had everything I needed. We had a brief conversation over the phone, and I enquired about everything at his home. He was so pleased to share that everything was in control and thanked me for remembering to ask about it. Kindness is like a magnet; it attracts kindness however sometimes you need a bigger magnet to receive it. You all are smart enough to understand the fine line between getting too personal and being kind enough to let someone know that you care for them. Never underestimate the kindness you are spreading and let it unfold its magic when you need it. Existence is outlandish; It is a delicate balance of various ecosystems that co-exist in the world. There is a constant battle of goodness and animosity and has been going on for ages.

Choose your side carefully and remember it takes courage to be kind. Being kind allows us to appreciate each other's values, circumstances, and differences. Acts can be forgotten but acts of kindness can never be overlooked. The Acts of kindness need not be grand and can be simply expressed by simple gestures. In fact, in the UK, #KindnessByPost is the UK's leading random acts of kindness exchange. I participated in the challenge multiple times, and it was so exciting to wait for an address to arrive, so that you can write a letter to a stranger at the given address. Similarly, someone would have received your address, and you wait for a letter to arrive. They set a theme to make it simpler for us to write a few sentences and sometimes send words of encouragement. I recall when I received my first letter as part of the Kindness challenge, the thrill to open the letter was limitless.

I had beautiful activity sheets with pictures of beautiful flowers sent out to me. I once received small cut-out squares, each with a different activity written on it, to help me practice being kind to myself and others every day!

That's just a small example of spreading kindness in the world to be the happiest person on the planet. Where would you look to start your kindness journey? What will be your one act of kindness every day, an act that is not a chore? How can you be kind in your conversations without being too obtrusive? Is there a cause in your life that allows you to express your kindness and nurture the trait in your future generations to follow? "A single act of kindness throws out roots in all directions, and the roots spring up and make new trees." Amelia Earhart's quote resonates well with the idea of spreading kindness no matter wherever you go, whatever you do. Remember to be kind!

Chapter 12
Fuel a Passion

One of my mentees, a promising engineer and passionate musician, Sanika, and I were talking about how her regular early morning schedule of practicing music makes her feel energised for the rest of the day. It was astonishing to see the efforts she was putting in to stay connected with her passion for music. According to her, it was worth the effort as it made it easier for her to enjoy the rest of her day and derive serenity.

"What time do you wake up every morning for your music practice"? I was intrigued by her passion for music.

"I wake up at 4:30 AM every day except Sunday to get ready by 5 AM. Music practice begins with warm-up, prayers, singing, playing sitar, and learning classical music from my mother. It continues until 6 AM before it is time for me to prepare for the day ahead in the college. I have been doing it since I was 8, and now it is a vital part of my day. Missing my practice session is like forgetting to add fuel to the car I drive—my life!". Sanika explained with intense emotions expressed in her eyes and voice as she walked me through her morning music practice routine. This great reflective statement about "fueling the car I drive" affirmed by a young engineer in a casual conversation, became my food for thought for the day. Sanika was fueling her passion every single day to drive forwards in her life.

"Have you found your purpose yet, Sanika?" I questioned, expecting a positive response as we continued our conversation.

"Yes, I believe my purpose is to spread awareness on the affluence of Indian Classical music, usher it to different parts of the world to allow others to experience the happiness I have been experiencing for years," she replied as her eyes glimmered.

"Well done, Sanika, you are on the right path. Keep up the good work! It is great to know that you have built clarity on your Purpose and Passion. Moreover, you haven't stopped there and continue to work towards your Purpose while you relish your Passion." I applauded her for her determination. She was following in the footsteps of many successful people who believed in themselves, pursued their passions, and let them to their Purpose—to be the North Star of their universe.

Sanika's exemplary actions are an inspiration for me, and it made me think: who is my inspiration? Who is the person who has shown great results with their actions and determination? The first name that comes to mind is of an excellent leader who displayed this inexorable passion for education and transformed it into his purpose of "Being a driving force in the success of India as a powerful nation," our Late President A.P.J. Abdul Kalam, famously known as the 'Missile Man of India.' He was one of the most successful scientists who led the missile program of India. Each time I am speaking to my mentees, I keep him in my mind and desire to follow his footsteps.

The passion with which he advocated for education and the success of young minds in India is unmatched. He was a firm believer in the power of pursuing one's passions and spent time with younger kids to inspire them to explore their passion for education. "If you want to shine like a sun, first burn like a sun." This quote from Kalam emphasises the importance of passion and hard work in achieving success. A well-summarized truth of our lives: pursuing our passions with dedication and determination will help us reach our goals and shine brightly in life.

Passion is something that you love, revere, and relish as you indulge in it. If you are in a job that lets you exercise your passion, you don't feel the burden of work anymore; the day seems to flow like a river. Purpose is what wakes you up every morning to exercise your passion in a way that you can bring out a positive difference in people's lives for the greater good. In fact, I have observed that it is common to see the role of a Chief People Purpose Officer or simply a Chief Purpose

Officer in large organisations; we don't see a Chief Passion Officer. Any thoughts on why? I personally learned that passion is what you truly relish, although your or your organisation's purpose is to provide a clear lens to make decisions that fasten it to its core values and beliefs. For example, a multinational Pharma GSK has a purpose defined on their website as "To unite science, technology and talent to get ahead of disease together." Similarly, Vodafone, a leading mobile service provider, has published a purpose: "Our purpose is to connect people, places, and things by enabling inclusive and sustainable digital societies – all for a better future." A well-defined purpose acts as a guiding star coupled with the values, beliefs, and a purposeful culture to endeavour for success.

Hence, the role of the Chief Purpose Officer looks to ensure that purpose is exhibited throughout an organisation and is embedded in whatever they do. To cement it further, the culture of the company reminds the employees to drive towards the Purpose powered by their Passion. Thus, building on Sanika's thought for us to drive our car, leading us forward in life guided by our purpose or the GPS, must be fueled by our very passion to make it a success. The principle is the same, irrespective of whether it is your personal or professional setting, the only subtle difference being who sets the Purpose. In your personal lives, you need to connect with your passion and explore your Purpose, whereas in your professional lives, your organisation defines a purpose that allows you to exercise your passion by being part of their journey.

Passion and Purpose are like two sides of a coin; they complement each other. On one hand, individuals and organisations cannot fructify their purpose without passion, and on the other, passion without an objective purpose is like an inflated balloon left with its end open. If you are a fitness or science enthusiast, Purpose is like the red fiber muscle of your body—they keep you going on and on. Passion is like the white fiber muscles that impart you with short and sudden bursts of energy.

The minor landmark successes act as a refueller as you run towards your goal. Well, I must mention an inspirational fictional character here; have you watched or heard of "Winnie the Pooh"? Winnie's passion for honey drives his middling life in a jungle to adventures with a strong desire to find honey every single day to calm his rumbling tummy. Imagining Winnie without his Passion for 'Hunny,' as he lovingly addresses honey, would be catastrophic. It is difficult to imagine what will get Winnie out of his bed to get ready to set out on his journey towards his Purpose of "Having unlimited stock of Hunny for life." Or if he didn't have this purpose, would he be so passionate about Hunny? It is time for us to ponder what is that "Fire in the belly," aka Passion, that pushes us to be a better version every single day to keep delivering towards our Purpose.

Do you know your passion and your purpose yet? If your answer is no to either part of the question, we are at a perfect moment to use the self-discovery exercises that were defined in previous chapters. To unravel your passion, mix your self-discovery with education, experience, and exposure. Further, the more you expose yourself to new people, ideas, activities, opportunities, and challenges, the better you will be able to articulate what fuels you and where you would like to drive to. Self-reflection in your journal is a great tool to endow you with the knowledge of what galvanises you or what activities you look forward to. To make it more interesting, you can observe your partner, kids, or peers to get a reading of what their passion is.

I have always found it to be super-energising to have a chat over a cup of coffee with different people to hear about their professional journeys and what excites them every day at work. I thrive on these communications to refuel my passion to write, blog, and, with time, I have created a purpose for me— 'Creating Happy, Hearty, and Healthy mindsets and making the world a beautiful place.' Are you fueling your passion with learning and successes already? Let's talk about it in our next chapter: how you can learn from your everyday experiences as you passionately work towards your purpose. Right now, I am off to complete my conversation with Sanika to learn from her experiences as she is learning on her journey to a purpose fueled by her passion for music.

Chapter 13
Every Day is an Opportunity to Learn

I continued my conversation with Sanika and asked her, "Why is it so important for you to practise your music regimen daily?"

"As I explained earlier, I absolutely enjoy it while it creates an opportunity for me to learn, too. I practise punctiliously to improve on what I have learnt earlier and learn more about music. There have been days when I had to unlearn a few things merely because it was essential to unlearn them to be able to learn something new," Sanika attempted to explain her connection with her passion and how it was associated with her everyday learning.

I couldn't agree more, and a quote that I saw on the internet came to my mind:

"Knowledge is when you learn something new every day. Wisdom is when you let something go every day." - Ralph Waldo Emerson.

Basically, Sanika was not just acquiring knowledge by practising music, her passion; nonetheless, she was also getting wiser in the whole progression. Impressive, sounds like killing two birds with one stone. We all have various opportunities every day to explore, learn, and gather experience; it is about how much we are willing to invest in our passion to lead a purposeful life. For me, writing every day is my attempt to stay connected with my passion and purpose. Each time I wish to write, I either discover myself better, or I end up researching, reading varied books, news, and informational articles to enrich my knowledge on the subject. If I go back in time, in my tenure as a technical trainer, I truly enjoyed writing and taking notes before my training sessions. As I prepared for my training, I had to go through a lot of content to ensure I had a good understanding of the topics I would be training the participants on.

These training sessions were so unique; even when I entered the training room thinking I had prepared well, someone would ask a question that required more research and deeper understanding. My job taught me to learn and, of course, unlearn as I acquired deeper knowledge on the subject, clarifying the misconceptions. My learning journey didn't end there, and I continue to learn every day, seizing opportunities. Being a lifelong learner has its benefits and can only be achieved by a growth mindset. One must constantly look out for ways in which they can enhance their knowledge and expand their mindset.

Another interesting aspect is to accept each other's differences to learn what each one brings to the table. In my current team, we are a group of people working for the same client. Although I have a limited scope that I must deliver, I make constant efforts to learn from my peers so that I can expand on 'what I know'. Similarly, I schedule connections with my peers who are working on similar clients from a similar industry to explore their learnings and experiences that can be useful for me and my client to discover. That's everyday learning from my professional life; besides, we all can learn from our own professional lives by being more receptive to knowledge from other sources. We all walk different paths in life; however, learning is available to all of us to imbibe. The learning may originate from our personal or professional environments as we continue to thrive in them every single day. Personally, I derive a lot of inspiration from sports that I play, watch, or do both.

As of now, the Wimbledon Tennis Championship is on in the UK, and as a tennis fan, I am impressed to see how the tennis players must learn and adapt as they are playing the match on the grass court. They practice almost every day to maintain their fitness and give their best shot on the court. There are possibilities wherein they play against an opponent they have never played before. The mindset that they have at their disposal is to learn everything about their opponent's game so that they enter the court prepared. Learning is crucial here, and it continues as long as we live; be it on court or off court, but we all are on a learning path in our respective fields. How? We learn from our family members, colleagues, people we meet, friends, our pets, nature, the internet, and social media. It can be qualified as unconscious learning, whereas if we take out time specifically to learn a subject, sport, etc., that's conscious learning. There is no set rule for what the right mix of these two types of learning; rather, what is of utmost importance is that you prioritise your own learning and continue it every day.

Here are a few steps you can take to foster learning every day in your schedule:

A simple and easy way to learn is to ask the question 'Why'. Example: I was asked by a team member to provide some data in a spreadsheet, but I made it a point to understand the full context before I mindlessly provided the data. Make it a habit to get closer to the context before giving solutions.

Carve out time in your schedule to invest in something you are passionate about- Dance for 20 minutes in the afternoon or read on the technology websites about your topics of interest to build a view of where the market is heading.

Listen carefully to the conversations you have throughout the day. Pay attention to listening to experiences that your friends and family share. There is so much hidden learning in these stories.

Take time to identify your hobbies, what sparks interest and pursuing them regularly can be a great start for your everyday learning journey.

Do not let age or any other aspect be a barrier to your learning. Make it a point to learn without any boundaries. Remember, the goal is to be a better version of you.

One important aspect to remember is that the results from learning are not instant. My daughter wanted to improve her handwriting, and on the very first day after writing 7 lines, she made a comment that she didn't see any improvement. After a conversation, I convinced her to continue practicing handwriting for a few more days. In fact, I designed a reward chart to reward her on the days she practiced. Days turned into weeks, and it became a habit for her to write a page practicing handwriting. Soon, it was parents evening at her school.

We accompanied her to school to discuss her performance with her class teacher, Mrs. Stevens.

The opening comment from her was, "Tanishka is a role model, and I am impressed by the improvement she has shown in her handwriting!" Our jaws dropped, but Tanishka had a wide smile celebrating the fruits of her weeks of practicing. The feedback from her class teacher reassured her of the value of everyday practice. Tanishka was fortunate to be rewarded to keep going with her practice to excel; we, as grown-up individuals, need to discover our own rewards or simply remind ourselves of our end goal. We must be patient with learning as it takes more than a day; rather, it is an everyday contribution to learn and excel. So, what did you learn today?

Chapter 14
Challenge Yourself

Recently at work, one of our senior managers, Chris, messaged the team: "Team nominations for the most awaited event of the year are out. I challenge you to nominate yourself as a speaker on any topic this year!" So, this is a massive event that brings together thousands of Sales colleagues from our organisation across the globe in one city for 4 days. I understand that it is not easy to get a speaker spot in this event as your topic must meet the requirements, and speakers who have spoken before and proven themselves have more chances to be successful. Odds were low, but my colleague Jas and I, from the same team, accepted the challenge. A one-word reply to a message felt so powerful. "Done," I replied to Chris's message about the challenge. Jas replied, "Challenge accepted, Chris!" There was a feeling that the first step towards personal development had been taken and brought a sense of accomplishment with it. We don't know yet if we will be speaking at this event; however, we are pleased with the fact that we stood up to the challenge. That was the professional life challenge situation handled well, and then my daughter arrived back from school.

After a brief chat with her about her day at school, she boasted how she could hula-hoop while walking and challenged me if I could hula-hoop only for 60 seconds while standing in one spot. Let me tell you, this was not my sweet spot. I declined the challenge outrightly, but Tanishka replied- "So are you going to give up, even before trying?". Wisdom exuded from her as she made this statement. For the next 30 minutes, I was hula-hooping in the garden hula-hooping, trying to meet the 60-second' mark. I managed to deliver the challenge almost a week later after a little practice and grit. It must be evident by now that challenges are everywhere, looking for us to come out of our comfort zone.

Challenges are an inevitable part of our life. We just use different names in our personal and professional lives. Think of the time you started schooling, when you had to learn to speak, write, and understand a language. The first step was to learn the alphabets, building words using alphabets, creating sentences using words, writing paragraphs using sentences, and it continued. What our teachers at school did was simple; they introduced a new challenge as we excelled in understanding and solving the first one. See, we've been exposed to challenges at a very early age, but they were not always referred to with the same name. So, what do we get out of these challenges? We discover, we learn, and we grow as individuals. The human brain enjoys challenges, as they have an element of uncertainty and problem-solving. It is fantastic for our brain muscles to flex and use different parts of our brain.

Research indicates that if we do not present new, surprising facts, information our brain power consequently starts deteriorating. In fact, I have noticed that our pet dog Ferro, absolutely loves challenges. He gets bored if not challenged with a game of fetch or the collection of dog puzzles he has. Instead of handing him treats, he must solve the dog puzzle challenges by sliding and twisting the blocks to uncover the treats. I believe he also enjoys the appreciation he receives after successfully revealing and consuming the treats. Challenging yourself is not always stress-free, but the rewards are worth it. When you step out of your comfort zone and accept challenges, you push past your confines and expand your horizons. The world has enough boundaries and let's not create boundaries in our minds to limit us. What is more interesting is that sometimes we have to look for challenges to grow whereas many are presented with challenges due to their financial or other constraints. There are inestimable examples in the history wherein great scientists, leaders, celebrities or successful authors have risen despite their struggles.

Benjamin Franklin, one of the founding fathers of America and a great physicist, was one of the seventeen children his father had from two wives. Despite his great interest in education, his parents couldn't afford to send him to school to pursue education. He gave up schooling at the age of 10 and educated himself through his voracious reading skills, alongside the job he did for his survival. India's ex-president A.P.J. Abdul Kalam used to study underneath a streetlight as there was no electricity at his home. Vincent Van Gogh, a famous Dutch painter, painted 2,100 artworks during his lifetime but sold only one. While he was alive, he struggled with his mental health. He rose above those challenges to continue producing paintings in the desire for a masterpiece. Today, he has a permanent art collection displayed in a museum named after him, and his paintings are the most sought-after and exclusive to own. Challenges bring out the best within us. We discover ourselves better as these experiences from the challenges we partake in help us grow as individuals, too.

When was the last time you experienced a scenario of uncertainty, difficulty level was high, and you had to make full use of your muscle power to find a solution to it?

Wait a minute, promising to wake up early and do yoga meditation and not keeping up the promise doesn't qualify as a challenge. On the contrary, you've declined the challenge to wake up earlier than your usual time and do something that doesn't qualify as part of your current daily routine. It may sound unbelievable, but I didn't learn to swim and drive until my late thirties. However, these challenges further add to my self-confidence. As we alluded to it in the previous chapters, it is crucial to find opportunities to learn every day. These challenges are our segue to learning a new subject or a skill by motivating us to look beyond our usual strengths and comforts.

A mantra that I live by is "Challenges open a new dimension in our personality and exalt our thinking, and one must accept it." It is great to be comfortable, but it is true that being too comfortable in our lives is as good as a walk in the same park every day. Imagine walking in the same park every single day. Wouldn't it be a great exercise for your mind and body if you could enjoy a walk in a new park where you've never been? Wouldn't it be awesome if you could run instead of walk? These small challenges and achieving them successfully add to our contentment and confidence. What will be your next challenge? A few random ideas for your next challenge: start writing in a diary, practice gratitude, learn to ride a horse, mountain climbing, snowboarding, snorkeling, prepare for your first marathon, or read a book!

Chapter 15
One Step at a Time

Ever wondered why we don't learn writing and speaking sentences directly? Why do we go to primary school before we can get to secondary school? To me, it seems like a gradual progression in our learning abilities, starting from basic and intermediate levels and moving to a professional level. It seems to be a universal rule to successfully build the foundations of the knowledge we wish to acquire before we can get comfortable with the subject. I recall as I was developing my speaking skills and getting over my stage fright, there were opportunities to participate in numerous competitions. Once, I nominated myself to speak on the topic of 'Genetics play a crucial role in defining our personality.' The speech was to be 15 minutes long and would be followed by a series of questions on the topic of genetics. You may think, so what? The interesting part here was that I knew nothing about genetics as the topic had yet to be introduced in the school. Probably in the spirit of taking challenges a bit too far, my science teacher supported me. She helped me with a write-up for this interschool competition.

We ended up with eight pages worth of content for me to cram. For the Q&A round, she prepared a couple of questions and seated a few of my fellow schoolmates in the audience so that I could answer familiar questions. On the day, I did well in the speech part, but when it came to the Q&A round, it was obvious that my knowledge was superficial. I had not understood the concepts and crammed the speech. The judges did recognise my talent for speaking with an appreciation certificate; however, I didn't win a prize. Well, I didn't lose anything, but it didn't seem fair to participate for the sake of participation.

Next challenge, I nominated myself for a topic— 'Human Body is a Marvel'— that I understood well, had studied in school, and could go over in detail. I could clearly experience a feeling of ease and how the ideas were flowing naturally rather than cramming them. Since I wasn't confident in 'Genetics,' I couldn't feel it or contribute my perspective; however, the latter gave me the opportunity to be more confident and share. One step at a time! I jumped to Genetics—an advanced science topic on genes—before I could understand the human body and its life processes. That's a clear reason why we learn to write alphabets before we can write words and sentences!

The above approach is helpful in breaking complexity or difficult situations. Most of the time, panic sets in when we overthink and create a mental picture of a pile of tasks to be done. While we do that, we send multiple signals to our brain at the same time about the numerous activities that await before our goal can be achieved. Instead of that, if we could break down the steps and assign a timeline to it, we can simplify for our brain to process which one needs to be prioritised. So, take a deep breath, sit down with your favourite drink and write down your plan. I have shared it in previous chapters, too, Writing is a bliss. It allows your brain to share the load by writing it down on paper or your electronic device. Speaking of panic set in, the first story that comes to mind is of my eldest sister- Sumita (Sumz); my niece Nik decided to get married, and we had a year to prepare for a traditional Indian wedding with modern customisation as per my niece's likings. The day Sumz received the news with a confirmed date, she was a different person: impatient, anxious and a bit lost.

Being a single mother and having a grand wedding to be planned was causing troubles, as she was playing all the events and requirements in her head. My niece, Nik sensed it and ordered a wedding planner for her to take notes, basically write down all her worries, so that we all knew where she would do with a little help. This simple gesture from Nik eased her worries as she could prioritise and visualise the tasks she had to accomplish. It allowed her to take one step at a time! A perfect way to ease her mind as she jotted down her long to-do list guided by the prompts in the wedding planner. Now each time she finished a task or delegated to someone; she could strike it off from her list of things. The wedding journal became her best friend, and she finally parted with it after all the payments for the wedding arrangements were made. Sumz felt so much in control in the months before the wedding, in contrast to how she responded to the responsibility of planning a wedding on day one.

The same approach works well at work too. Every day before you start answering the emails, take the first 15 minutes to plan your day with what you would like to accomplish by the end of the day; the key tasks, meetings or preparations for the meetings. As you whizz through the day finishing these tasks, strike them off your list to take one step towards your objective of a successful day that you defined at the start.

I sometimes use sticky notes and write down the tasks to be accomplished, pin them to a board and remove them as I achieve them. Imagine the feeling of walking through a strawberry farm with an empty basket; the goal is to fill up this basket. How would you fill it? Will you pluck all the strawberries at the same time? One strawberry at a time seems more practical. One step at a time, slowly and steadily, will take you towards your goal if you continue with the right focus. When we are working, every morning, we start with an empty basket with a goal to fill it with our accomplishments. Follow the 'One step at a time' mantra to have your bucket filled with accomplishments leading to joy.

There is no doubt that at times, we are under immense pressure, and we intend to finish everything at once. These are the times when it becomes more critical to identify the series of tasks that can be completed, the order of priority, and the time required to finish these. Years ago, I read 'Eat the Frog,' a book by Brian Tracy, who explained the method of 'Eat the Frog' to avoid procrastination by completing one hardest task every morning and then moving on to other tasks.

However, this process must be repeated every day. The advantage is that it encourages you to self-define your agenda, identify your difficult tasks, and the time required for planning. This leads to a sense of accomplishment and contentment. Additionally, it sets the momentum for the day with success. This method sounds difficult as one is encouraged to accomplish the most difficult task, although it is the best way to take a step towards something that will create high impact upon completion and leaves no room for procrastination. This idea is believed to have originated with Mark Twain when he said: "If it's your job to eat a frog, it's best to do it first thing in the morning. And if it's your job to eat two frogs, it's best to eat the biggest one first." A profound thought, as it is our natural tendency to run away from challenges; it is quite possible that most of us might find it hard to focus on getting the most difficult task out the door.

The above-explained method encourages us to challenge ourselves to bring a change in our way of working by starting off with the biggest and most high-impact task in hand. Well, that's not any different from how a child grows. The first five years are the years when the child needs the most attention and is dependent on his parents for his day-to-day activities. We don't give up thinking about the days that would follow a child's birth. We take one step at a time; as we grow, we gather experiences that add wisdom to our next steps in life. There are so many possibilities in this universe we cannot possibly have an answer for every scenario. However, we can prepare ourselves to learn at every step of our life, gather these experiences; apply them in our lifetimes and as we continue to progress, we take one step at a time, each time with a wiser, stronger and confident selves.

Chapter 16
Record Your Successes

The last few years, I have been doing several amazing things at work that would have contributed towards my personal and professional development; however, I missed highlighting them whenever it was time for the annual reviews in the organisation. I had been doing this for a few years until I met a wonderful coach, Dan, at work. It was a privilege to have 1:1 coaching session with him to get clarity on various topics and get a steer on how to navigate complex situations at work. In one of these sessions, I questioned Dan, "How can I ask for a promotion, as it doesn't come to me naturally? I find it hard to ask for it. There is a fear that if my manager asks me why we should get you promoted, I might not have the right answer to justify my request." I asked with great curiosity and a strong desire to get an answer to my bewilderment.

"If you are delivering the outcomes that are expected of you, and as far as I know, you are involved in various stretch assignments, that implies you are delivering much more than you are expected to do. What is the hesitation in asking for a promotion?" Dan looked befuddled.

"I totally agree. The challenge is when it is that time of the year, and we are discussing my successes, I remember only the latest ones and struggle to call out the efforts that I made throughout the year. The result being I don't feel confident that I have delivered enough to ask for a promotion," I explained frantically to Dan as I was getting restless thinking about the upcoming annual review.

"Ah, you've got it. The answer is simple. You must start a success journal to record every success, effort, and key event for your reference. When it is that time of the year, you can easily export your accomplishments from your success journal on your computer to the employee review portal. This will save you a lot of time, effort, and frustration in the future. Create sections in your success journal, such as personal and professional development, to make it more succinct. Once you get used to it, you will never miss mentioning your successes all around the year. The biggest advantage will be, as you note your successes in the journal/file, you will unconsciously appreciate your own efforts and will be motivated by your small wins. We all need minor landmarks, as shared in the previous chapter, as we take one step at a time. These regular feeds in the success journal will create a stairway to success at the year-end for you, as you will be more equipped to articulate your full success story."

"Thanks Dan, I will get started today. What a great plan!" I expressed gratitude with an overwhelming feeling of joy of finding a resolution or pathway to my success.

I started my success journal that day, and the first entry in my personal development was-"Regular bi-weekly coaching sessions with Dan". That's my story, how about you all? Do you record your successes yet or wait for the day when you have a conversation with your organisation to discuss your future growth? Being proactive is my mantra when it comes to my personal and professional growth. Henceforth, I keep my success journal up to date to be used at any time to highlight the efforts that I am making to grow professionally and personally. Example: My success in being able to successfully swim or completing an elementary-level certificate in the Spanish language might not contribute directly to my professional growth but is an important aspect of my personal growth.

It is key to take notes of actions that you would like to take to grow not just professionally but personally, too. There are numerous personal development templates available online that can be adopted to define our success journey. However, one must not forget about this Personal Development Plan after filling it out once. It must be a living document that should be used throughout the year with your manager or mentors to guide you. In fact, this is excellent to take a stalk of how you are charting towards the milestones you have defined for your success. We cannot expect to be guided or delivered with well-carved development plans for ourselves or hire someone else to narrate our success story. We must be our own brand ambassador to narrate our success story in a way that reverberates throughout the organisation, not once but many times.

Let me share a glimpse of how I have adopted the habit of recording success in my daily schedule.

1. Friday evenings, before I leave my desk, I take a note of 3 things that I accomplished during the week, or I am proud to be associated with in my success journal in Microsoft One note. I ensure these notes are dated and are brief enough for me to understand.
2. I use these Star stickers that I stick on a day of the week that is special for me, as I have accomplished something on the day. These stars encourage me to get more just like a 'Kids reward programme".
3. In my bi-weekly conversation with my manager- I share a summary of my achievements and discuss with him how I achieved them or seek guidance on how I could achieve them.
4. After a successful event, conference, I ensure I do a LinkedIn Post, write-up so that I ensure my visibility inside and outside of my organisation to build more connections. It also serves as a reminder for me as to where I invested my time and energy, beyond the usual work.
5. If you work closely with customers; if your clients are pleased with your work, ensure you arrange to take written feedback that can be shared with your manager for his review and knowledge.

Similarly, the clients can be your internal stakeholders too. If you have excelled in a particular project, make it a point to take feedback from your stakeholders.

After all, you have worked hard to be successful. One doesn't achieve success by chance, it takes a lot of hard work beyond talent. Thomas Edison tried 1000 times before inventing a bulb, it wasn't just serendipity! Hard Work combined with Passion led him there. You are on your journey to discover something that your heart desires. Why give it up? Ensure you record through every step all the way.

Chapter 17
Financial Literacy Starts Early

During my engineering days, as I was in Mumbai on my own, time arrived for the first instalment of college fees. The college gave a very specific instruction to get a – Demand Draft of a certain amount in a couple of days. I was clueless on how to get one until I found someone who was going to a bank for the same. As I queued up in the bank to get a demand draft issued, I wondered if I had lived under a rock all this while. I knew about a 'cheque' but how did I miss the 'Demand Draft'? Are these two different? why a demand draft and not a cheque can be accepted by my college? I searched for answers in a desperate attempt to make myself- 'Financially literate'.

In the next two years, I learned so much about money, saving and managing expenses, and operating a savings account on my own. Initially, it wasn't easy for me to control my spendthrift habits; I was exhausting my monthly expenditure fund even before the month ended. It resulted in me calling home to request more funds or sometimes borrowing it from my uncle after a call from my dad, until one day, when I contacted my uncle to ask if my dad had contacted him to give me ten thousand Indian Rupees. He replied on the phone, "What do you do with your mom's hard-earned money?" as he broke into hysterical laughter.

I replied, "Nothing, sorry, I must go." I disconnected the call as I replayed the conversation in my head. This episode made me rethink if there was something amiss in my money management skills, and maybe it was the perfect time for me to pause, reflect, and redefine if there is a better way to manage my expenses with my allowance. The results were not exemplary, but gradually, I started developing more control over my urge to spend as I had a clear view of expenses planned against my monthly allowance. Basically, a question from my uncle turned the tables for me and compelled me to educate myself on money management, too. Today, when I think about it, the first thought that comes to mind is, "What if I was financially literate before I started my higher education? I could have saved trouble for my family with my demands for additional support."

For the same reason, we started 'Financial literacy' very early for Tanishka. We started with' Monopoly' to explain the finance basics and build her foundations on the subject. She learnt the value of money, the fact that there isn't an infinite supply, and a lot goes on to get money in the wallet. The house we live in also has a value associated with it, sometimes it is fully paid or maybe partially. We started a reward system for her, wherein we were able to encourage her to participate in daily chores like gardening, helping by taking her washed laundry to her room, folding and arranging, etc. We learnt this after moving to the UK that we must encourage kids to earn, spend and be independent at an early age. Any misbehaviour or excess screen time would lead to financial penalties. The profit, loss concept, and calculating the after-discount price while she shopped during sale season. We were also clear on one thing: that financial literacy must not be limited to learning about earning and saving money in a bank account.

Often, we associate financial literacy with knowing ways and means of saving money for the future. However, it has another dimension to it - knowing ways and means to supplement your income; how to generate multiple sources of income; how to create wealth and not just earn money. In the times of ever-increasing inflation, we cannot rely on salary incomes. The young kids must be taught to pursue hobbies and interests which can be an additional source of income. In an era of widespread social media presence, kids can be a blogger, have a podcast, and on one hand, earn revenue from it, while on the other, acquire confidence to be a public speaker.

With the right guidance, young adults can be taught about financial investment options to acquire additional sources of income. It also helps to build a spirit of entrepreneurship and responsibility. I recall, as a nine-year-old, my entrepreneurial skills were sparking, and with the help of my friend Shalu, we made colourful friendship bands. The idea was to sell them to earn money! We decided to use a table to display them in front of her dad's grocery store. It was a perfect plan until it was instantly killed by my family as they decided to buy all the friendship bands at once. I was thrilled as a kid, although when I analyse it today, it could have been a great opportunity to awaken the entrepreneur within me.

Most of us tend to do something similar with our kids, too. "Oh, I never had pink shoes when I was a kid; my child should have them," or "I don't want my child to be deprived of anything; he should have everything that's the best out there." We start living our childhood through them, forgetting about their only chance to make the best of their childhood. Everything is available in such abundance that they no longer have a drive to achieve more. The value of money diminishes when they see you buying stuff at the tap of your debit card or ordering from Amazon in one swipe. A while ago, I went out shopping with my daughter; she had a long list of things to purchase. "Mom, can I buy a few of these items?" she inquired— "only seven of these"—she looked into my eyes to get my approval. "Yes, with your money. If you are not carrying it, we can deduct it from your account," I replied as I casually walked inside the store.

Finally, she decided to buy only one item, and the other six items were dropped. This brought about another change; she self-nominated for the role of a cashier in a junior co-operative bank working with her school. She started saving the money she earned from the chores at home in the junior bank account. The school did a superb job of rewarding kids who regularly deposited money. It is super important for kids to realise the value of money, how to save, spend, and grow it. We, as parents, hold this responsibility to educate them on finance management through different ways to help them in building a healthy habit for life.

First and foremost, we should educate ourselves to become smart investors, cultivating healthy wealth-building habits that can be passed down to future generations. A question arises: How can we educate ourselves on the subject of financial management if we miss the boat of financial literacy at an early age? Before I answer, do you agree that we are never too old to learn? If you do, I recommend reading books on financial literacy. Start with "Investing for

Dummies" or "Corporate Finance for Dummies"; you can do a course on Udemy or, to get practical experience, start paying attention to your finances, bank accounts, and investments.

I recall my journey, when I realised that I had no plan for my earnings. How do I ensure that I save for emergencies? When will I invest in my own house? There were a million questions that needed answering. That's where I used my banking services provider to provide me with education on the investment options with short-term, long-term gain, and the shortcomings of different financial instruments. Earlier, I relied on the traditional financial investment modes like fixed deposits, savings bank accounts, recurring deposits, and mutual funds. Anything beyond it appeared alien to me. Slowly, I was developing wings through my efforts to educate myself on financial management, growth, and stability. In two years, I invested in my first house ever in the UK after spending enormous time understanding how the lending, payback, negotiation, insurance, taxation, and legal process work.

Buying my first house was a great milestone, an experience that made me more confident about my finances and financial knowledge. I could have a better conversation with my co-workers on the topic of housing, finance, etc. I had also realised by now that to operate in a corporate environment, it is imperative to have a basic understanding of corporate finance, financial terms, and the impact they have on the business. I recall it was in the 'Year of Pandemic'; I was desperately looking for financial advice. It was that time when I stumbled upon a podcast, "Girls That Invest", hosted by a young millionaire investor Simran Kaur and her friends. The episode that I tuned in to was on "How People are Retiring in their Thirties; Financial Independence Retire Early (FIRE)." What an interesting topic that was taking the financial industry by storm; the insights shared in this 40-minute episode were enlightening.

Ah, an idea danced in front of my eyes, so it is not just about Early Financial Literacy (EFL) but also Early Financial Independence (EFI). As I continued to listen to the podcast series, I further acquired knowledge on various financial concepts, Stock market investments, inheritance, start-ups, investing in real estate etc. This led me to invest further in real estate and become a first-time landlord. There has been no looking back since then, as I have been invested in enhancing my financial skills. My business language incorporates financial terms that I understand and are appreciated by the enterprise customers too. I have managed to develop an outlook that takes into consideration commercial aspects like- Capital Expenditure (CapEx), Operational Expenditure (OpEx), Return on Investment (RoI), Total Cost of Ownership (TCO), Net Present Value (NPV), Added Recurring Revenue (ARR), Earnings Before Interest Tax Depreciation and Tax (EBITDA) the list keeps growing with my experience, exposure and education.

Obviously, I will miss the FIRE target of retiring in my thirties, but there is still a hope to do better than the standard retirement age set by the government. Well, not going so far from now, we must ensure we understand the value of financial literacy; how it can accelerate our financial growth if we understand our finances. Let me inspire you with a quote that summarises the value of financial literacy extremely well.

"Financial literacy" is an important part of avoiding financial mistakes and planning for a strong financial future."- Tim Pawlenty, President and CEO, Financial Services Round Table.

Section 3
Social Interactions and Relationships

Humans are an integral part of a society that is built through numerous bonds and relations that we create. To thrive in this society, we must understand the value of relationships and strengthen them over the course of time. No doubt, once you have befriended yourself, created a discipline to adhere to, it is imperative that you expand your network and build meaningful connections. Building connections doesn't imply building a massive follower base on social media, rather it reflects the idea of being open to the disparate mindsets people have.

"Electric communication will never be a substitute for the face of someone who with their soul encourages another person to be brave and true."

– Charles Dickens

Chapter 18
Share Responsibility, Build Lasting Trust

Whenever I am traveling with my family or for work, I have a preferred hotel chain that I stay with. For simple reasons – I trust them to provide me with the comfort, security, and hospitality that I expect when away from my home. The hotel chain didn't insist that I should trust them; our experiences defined whether they could be trusted. Similarly, in a relationship between two or more, whether personal or professional, it is foundational to have trust. It doesn't matter if there is an inherent desire to be trusted by others involved; what matters is the experience that you are providing them. One needs to build strong foundations to be able to develop trusted relationships. The question arises: how do we have a strong foundation in any relationship? Is 'trust' a virtue that can be instilled in a relationship by either party, or is it something that one develops over time? Think of your 'trusted hairstylist,' 'trusted doggie daycare,' 'trusted bank'; we tend to put trust before everything that matters to us.

I do feel the word 'trust' is a bit overused and often misunderstood. The other day, while we were all chatting as a family, my daughter was busy looking down at her phone, her fingers all over the screen. This continued for some time as she seemed disengaged from our conversations. We tried getting her attention by asking her about her thoughts on the topic, and she half-heartedly participated in the conversation. She was disconnected.

I called her out again, this time— "Tanishka, I thought we were spending some time together. Could you please be here with us in the physical world?"—sternly reminding her of our existence.

"I am looking for this week's homework that I need to complete. You don't trust me, when I am on my phone." She walked away furiously before we could explain our intent. It isn't about trusting her but about ensuring she is surrounded by trustworthy people and being exposed to content that is right for her age. What trust was she referring to? I trust my own daughter; it is a matter of being responsible as a parent. I was delivering on the trust that she has entrusted to me as a parent to take care of her and guide her. As social media can be unfortified and dangerous, I was trying to protect her from exposure to negative influences. This wasn't the right time to follow her and explain my intent. I waited for a moment in the next few days, when she seemed to be receptive, to assure her of how much we both—her parents—love her; our clear intent to support her in her endeavours, and finally, 'No Phones' when spending time with family.

This simple encounter made me think, what does the word 'Trust' imply? Was I wrong in demanding my daughter's attention? Now, I had to earn her trust and make her feel that she was entrusted. Here comes the life lesson I learned to take: 'One step at a time.' I arranged for a shopping day for just the two of us to spend some time together. After long hours of hard work finding the right items to shop for, try, and buy, we decided to take a break. I was prepared to find a segue in the conversation to talk about 'Trust.' I clarified my stance the other day and explained to her how valuable it is for me to be entrusted by her, and I trust her with my eyes closed.

An open conversation with my daughter helped me assure her that she is trusted and reminded her that she can trust us to be by her side. It felt great to have a hearty conversation with her. We didn't demand trust from each other, but we were working in the direction of earning each other's trust despite the negative influences that may cause trepidation. Great, we did make some progress here, but that's not the only relationship I hold. We all have numerous relationships in our personal and professional lives that require Trust to sustain, and it is equally vital for us to earn trust to be effective.

Let's explore this aspect from a different perspective beyond just our personal lives. When it comes to our professional lives, we all have managers, and many of us are managers who are responsible for the growth of many individuals.

How do you earn trust as a leader? There have been various research articles on the prominence of trust in developing business relations. I was reading the Harvard Business Review's article - Begin with Trust, and it explains- "The Trust Triangle - Trust has three core drivers: authenticity, logic, and empathy. As per HBR's aforementioned article, People tend to trust you when they believe they are interacting with the real you (authenticity), when they have faith in your judgment and competence (logic), and when they feel that you care about them (empathy)." The article further describes the concept of 'Trust Wobble'; one of the Trust Drivers that can lead you to failure or a situation of mistrust. In many parent-child relationships, the 'Trust Wobble' might vary. If the child is unable to share his or her authentic self with you due to fear of how you would react, it can make it difficult for you as a parent to trust. Whereas if you are unable to empathise with your child by explaining the logic of your actions and reactions, trust cannot be built. Have you ever hoped to be trusted or been in situations where you experienced that you weren't trusted to take up more responsibility or a new role? Isn't it crucial to identify what was missing in the way you presented yourself? Is it the Authenticity - did you hide your real self, Logic - Did you sound full of yourself, your aspirations, and desires, or Logic - did they doubt your competency to be able to do that job role? If you can find the Trust Wobble out of these three, then you can work on strengthening the wobble to build a stable foundation. As trust doesn't flourish on shaky ground, trust itself is the strong foundation.

Recently, I had an experience that really brought these aspects to light for me. I applied for a role within my organisation. I was confident that I would be the best fit for the role. However, an external candidate was hired. This did leave me a bit clueless on – 'Why wasn't I trusted to deliver this job?'. I had two choices: to sulk from within about the situation or work it out with the hiring manager to understand what I could have done better to be successful. As I arranged a few calls with the hiring manager and the members of the group interview panel, I learned that I failed to display my business leadership skills, and my technical knowledge dominated my presentation. However, the role was being created specifically to find a business leader who could drive business outcome-led discussions. So, I missed hitting the nail or the 3rd element of the Trust Triangle – Logic.

Well, we learn from our lessons. This led me to a process wherein I started analysing the professional situations with my co-workers and key stakeholders that I work with. In my job, being in technical sales, it is crucial for me to build a trusted relationship with my customer counterparts. I give them technical advice that is in their best interest and delivers value for their investments. Every recommendation I make is well-backed by logic and reasoning for my customer to evaluate their final decision. Imagine if these recommendations were backed by no logic—it would be hard for anyone to receive them.

In the background, I must ensure that the groundwork is done to be able to elaborate and share as many details as are required to empower my customers to decide where to invest. Yes, I care for my organisation that has hired me, but I equally care for the customer who trusts us with their business to continue to believe in our solutions. This is earning trust in our professional lives and a bit on parenting. What about our partner? I would turn to the 'Trust Triangle,' and the answers lie within it. These relationships can experience a 'Trust Wobble' if we fail to empathise with our partner or just miss focusing on their needs. Sometimes, we forget to be our true authentic self, or certain toxic relationships do not allow us to be our real self. They are filled with pretentious behaviour to keep the relationship alive. Such relationships exist but do not persist as the core foundation of trust isn't strong enough.

Nonetheless, Trust is a commitment to be true to each other and stand by the promises that were made at the beginning of a personal or professional relationship. I recall, as a kid, how our parents preferred certain brands to be more trusted and continue to have these choices. The trust sometimes is passed on from one generation to another as you get exposed to these experiences at an early age. Trust isn't plucked from a tree or harvested from a field, it is a virtue that develops as one gets to know the other, believes in it, and appreciates the competence with care.

Trust is what a farmer exhibits in his field, believing it will produce a yield to feed his family. He puts his heart and soul into plowing, seeding, and watering the field to ensure it produces a great harvest when the season arrives. The crops in the field believe in the competence of the farmer, relying on him to be nurtured and harvested. It is mutual, even though the field cannot say it aloud. In our daily lives, when we decide to buy toothpaste of a certain brand over a thousand others, it is a small step toward building trust if the toothpaste delivers on its promises. The other day, I was thinking it is so adorable how our pet dog Ferro rolls onto his back, exposing his belly as he demands a belly rub from my daughter when she is back from school. After looking online about this behavior, I discovered it is common among dogs to show they trust you by bringing over their favorite toy, gazing into your eyes, or rolling onto their backs.

It is their language that expresses their love and trust in you; they trust to be with you when they are most vulnerable, in their sleep or while on their back. This is such an important facet of the relationship between the pet and the owner to develop a bond of trust. Profound, aren't we doing the same? If you give it a thought, if we want someone to trust us, we have to show them we trust them even when we are most vulnerable. Have you shown your vulnerable self to your partner or family? Have you cried in front of your best friend or shared the good news you've been waiting for years with someone you trust? If we trust someone, we are pleased to share our successes, failures, thoughts, possessions, and time with them. However, it further depends on whether it is a personal or a professional relationship, as the boundaries may vary in these relationships. We trust our almighty, our revered deities, partners, best friends, and kids with a strong belief that we will be guided; they will be there to catch us when we fall.

The whole world is operating with a sprinkle of Trust in everything. We must be there with the best of us, with their best interests at the center of our relationship. The good thing is we don't have to express ourselves like Ferro by rolling on our backs for a belly rub; history has shown numerous gestures and symbols to express trust. Example: Various scholars date the origins of the handshake to ancient Greece. It was more than a gesture; by extending one's right hand, strangers could exhibit that they weren't in possession of a weapon. Some historians believe the handshaking gesture came later, in the Middle Ages, when knights would shake hands vigorously to reveal any hidden weapons, such as a dagger up the sleeve.

How smart, right? It is crucial to note that to trust someone, you need to show who you are, what you feel, and why you are here to establish a trusted relationship. Think of hiding your discomforts from your doctor, details from your lawyer, weaknesses from your teacher, dreams from your partner, and appreciation from your kids. As you get more comfortable in sharing your whole self with the required aspects of the different relationships we experience at home and work, you empower yourself with the talent to further strengthen trust relationships.

I recall my friend Ananya was furious about a last-minute assignment that she was asked to complete with little or no help. The assignment was handed over to her manager by his manager, and he simply passed it on to her. He had a stringent timeline and was sure that Ananya would deliver it without fail.

"How can someone be so emotionless? I had planned a week at my parent's place with the kids. The kids were so disappointed," Ananya shared her agony.

"It's painful to move around personal commitments, and kids get disheartened with rejigs," I added.

"Exactly, it was difficult for all of us at home, and the assignment was so intense," Ananya shared her experience.

"It would have been nice if at least my manager had asked me if I needed any support to complete it. A call from him to check the direction of progress or guide me would have encouraged me."

"It sounds to me that your manager totally entrusted you with this assignment. However, a little compassion and effort to share the burden would have turned the deadline's negative influence into a positive one." There was an agreement on the subject. Ananya was delighted to know that she was entrusted with the task because her manager believed in her competence, but he missed empathising and explaining the logic behind why it needed to be completed so urgently that she had to rejig her whole life. That's where context helps; rather than asking someone to just fill in a spreadsheet with their responses, if we care to explain the objective behind it, research has proven that better results are expected. This highlights the fact that it is crucial to share the burden; excellence in the art of delegation is an asset. However, one must not forget the basics of being a trusted leader when delegating.

A regular assurance of your support, availability, and guidance must be provided to ensure the individual who has received your delegated task doesn't feel like they are the only person lifting the mountain. I recall how I learned to ride a bike. Initially, my dad would hold my bike by the steering handle to keep me steady and moving as I pedalled the bike. Then, as I improved with steering, he would hold the bike from behind to make sure I maintained my balance. He did it for 2-3 days, and one day, when I looked behind me, there was no one, and I was riding a bike on my own. My dad had let go of my bike a while back while I believed he was holding me; it gave me the confidence and assurance to keep going on the bike. The moment I realised he was not behind me, and I was on my own, panic set in, and I fell off the bike. That's human psychology for you. We need assurances in life to keep going or to do challenging things. We need someone to trust us, believe in our capabilities, feel our pain, think of our welfare, and we can lift mountains.

Are you one of those who is sharing the weight as you entrust others with challenges?

Few exercises to develop deeper Trusted relationships:

- Choose an activity, sport, or baking project that you and your partner or child would like to try for the first time. If this is an activity that you do not trust your child or partner to do on their own, instead of doubting them, look for ways you can help them experience it with your encouragement and support. Example: I wanted to try a high rope challenge in an adventure park during one of our corporate events and had doubts that I could do it. My teammates not only encouraged me but also looked out for me throughout the challenge to ensure I finished it safely.
- Take a fun quiz with your partner or kids to answer the question: "3 things they would trust you to do perfectly, 3 things they trust you cannot handle, and 3 reasons why they trust you." Now, here's your cue—you can

get a sneak peek into the areas or activities you need to explore to double down on trusted relationships or the relationships that are valuable to you. I did this with my family, and my daughter had one point under "What she trusts that I cannot handle": "Mom, you cannot assemble furniture!" The next time we ordered a piece of furniture, I made sure to join both my husband and daughter in the furniture assembly experience while we worked as a team!

Chapter 19

One Mouth, Two Ears: Words Are Power

Early in my pre-sales career, I secured a meeting with an important stakeholder in an allocated account. I was eagerly looking forward to this meeting and prepared a list of points that I would share. I met him and shared all the points that I had noted down in the allocated meeting time. What a feat! Well done, Priyanka! I thought as I returned to my office. Later in the day, I had a debrief meeting with my manager, Paul. I enthusiastically shared how efficiently I managed my time to share everything I had noted down.

"That's great. It's a breakthrough to get time with a key stakeholder. What did you learn from him?" Paul asked to better understand the conversation.

"The Customer wasn't very vocal; he mostly nodded or concurred," I replied, wondering if I had missed the opportunity to ask him something.

"It wasn't a conversation in that case, he was a great listener. Did you listen to him in that meeting?" Paul made a point as he looked straight into my eyes.

"Sorry, I don't follow you. I thought it was a great meeting!" I fumbled as I tried to make sense of his comments.

"I will say it is a missed opportunity, if we are unable to listen to him about what his role entails, his key priorities, challenges and how we can help him to be successful in that role. Listening is a skill, and active listening is an asset to have in one's stride. Don't be disheartened, we will work on developing these skills together. I am learning every single day!" He assured me that we would get there with continuous efforts to sharpen our listening skills.

"Thank you, that's enlightening. You have totally changed my perception of that meeting!" I expressed gratitude for sharing his valuable experience, even though I felt a bit baffled.

The conversation with Paul was difficult and comforting both at the same time. I wasn't expecting this response from him, but I felt comforted by the fact that he gave me critical feedback to be a better version of myself. Paul added, "I believe sometimes it is our nerves that we cannot stop speaking, however redundant our point might be. I have witnessed myself in a few situations in my early career wherein my words rushed through the floodgates like restrained water. I would speak very fast and just wouldn't stop speaking on the topic to make my point. Thanks to a wonderful coach whom I met during those days, he identified this behavior in me. I still remember his exact words, 'Paul, why are you afraid of silence? Own it, embrace it.'"

"Can silence be a sign of failure to respond?" I questioned Paul.

Paul explained, "No, silence is not a sign of failure; it must be used appropriately. Use brief pauses, silence when you are conversing, saying no words at all. It exudes confidence. One must allow their listeners to absorb; they won't object to the pause. The pause can be brief, a few seconds, like rhythmically catching a breath in a swimming stroke rather than swimming with lungs filled with air at once to last the lap." He continued, "Remember the movie Spiderman when Peter Parker gained his powers? He was told and asked to remember for life: with great power comes great responsibility. The ability to speak and use our words appropriately is a power, and we must use it sensibly. Wishing you good luck, Priyanka, for your future conversations." Having said that, my manager rushed to attend his next meeting.

Thereafter, during my product presentations, I started experimenting with pauses. Whenever I briefly paused for a few seconds, there were instances where my audience would ask a question, or I further probed them if there were any questions for me. While they scrambled their brains for a question, I would catch a breath and direct my energy in the right direction: get control of the content in a presentation. It was a great tip for me to further enhance my communication skills and improve my listening skills at the same time. On the other hand, I started delivering effective presentations wherein it was no longer a one-way presentation but a two-way dialogue to articulate the message succinctly.

Learning from Paul wasn't all; there is another teacher in my life, my mother, who has taught me about the importance of listening. As a kid, after coming back from school, I would insist on her to tell me a story. Mom, being a teacher, always had lots of moral stories, and I would patiently listen to these stories, waiting for her to ask me, "What did you learn from the story?" giving me a gaze, scanning for answers in my eyes. I would gather words to construct a meaningful explanation. Mom always replied by encouraging me and responding with, "Good girl, you are an attentive listener. The moral of the story is…" I felt rewarded when I got appreciation from my mom for my attentiveness. I recall once I accompanied her to school due to a personal emergency. I sneaked into her classroom. There was a big blackboard with a lot of details written on it, starting from date, attendance, subjects, etc. In one corner, there was a quote: "One mouth, two ears." I was intrigued by the underlying meaning. During her lunch break, I asked, "Mom, what did the quote written on your classroom's blackboard mean?" She laughed at first, "Oh, you noticed! It means God has given us one mouth and two ears for a reason, and these must be used in the right proportion. Example: If you must serve water from a jug, can you serve it from an empty one? To fill it up, you need water from a tap or another water source. Likewise, our mouth needs knowledge before we can pour words. Hmm, what do you think, *beta*?" Mom gently patted my back, encouraging me to think.

"Yes, Mum, you're right, we need to fill the jar first," I replied confidently, thinking what an easy question but still struggling to understand the relevance to my question.

"Wonderful. Now think of your two ears as taps that are filling you up with knowledge to process, so that you can pour it in the form of words from your mouth when required. So, two ears, one mouth. Got it, my smarty pants?"

"Woah! This is a great example, Mum. I need to listen more and speak when required with the right knowledge."

"Yes, you don't have to speak for the sake of speaking. It is best to stay quiet and listen when you do not have the right knowledge on a subject. You must speak to ask as many questions as possible to learn, if appropriate for that forum but do not speak because you want to show your presence in the room. Well don't worry, you did the right thing by asking this question at the right time and right place." Mum smiled at me, pleased that she could clarify my doubts with ease.

Another important lesson for me is to value words and to spend them sparingly. This reminds me of a childhood story - a tortoise, Mr. Toto, lived in a pond along with the other birds. Two of the cranes were his dear friends, Mr. & Mrs. Crane. They enjoyed their sunny afternoons and evenings together, and Mr. Toto entertained them with his endless stories. Life was beautiful in and around the pond until there was a drought, and the pond dried up. There was no source of water for miles. Many of the wildlife started dying, and others who could relocate started in the hope of greener pastures.

Mrs. & Mr. Crane were off to a distant pond to restart their life and were sad to leave Mr. Toto behind. However, Mr. Toto had other plans. He proposed that if the two cranes could hold a stick between their beaks, he could hold the stick in his mouth. Mrs. Crane was thrilled that they would be able to save their dear friend. Mr. Crane, knowing his friend well, warned him of the risks involved because if Mr. Toto, who was an incessant speaker, opened his mouth to utter a single word, it would be Mr. Toto's first and last flight.

Mr. Toto assured the Cranes that he was smart enough to know when not to speak. The journey began, and soon Mr. Toto was soaring in the sky as other birds looked at the trio in amazement. Commendations for the Cranes started pouring in from all around. It was a bit unsettling for Mr. Toto, but he reminded himself of the consequence of speaking. Then a comment from a parrot praising the Cranes for their intelligence—a fantastic idea—was unbearable for Mr. Toto. He opened his mouth to say, "It was…" A thud led him to his last breath on the ground. He failed to save his life by not quietly executing his own plan—a plan that would have given him a new life experience. He was pushed by birds, strangers who knew nothing about him or his life. Mr. Toto gave up his life for no one and nothing.

Do you know Mr. Toto inside you? Mr. Toto who is so eager to shout out to everyone that this was my idea, and it becomes so important that you forget the success of your team is your success. Do you speak out loud just to reiterate that it is you who got them there rather than being a part of a team? This story is profound; it has so many morals to derive from it. Yes, words are power, and Mr. Toto exercised his power in the wrong place and at the wrong time. I have fallen into this trap so many times in my personal and professional life. Sometimes I am competing with my own partner to show off to my daughter that I love her more. Funnily enough, she is a smart kid who always responds with "Thank you, Mumma, Papa!"

What if we leave behind our egos, share the load with the team, actively listen to the ideas, and share our wisdom concisely when required? The question arises: how do we harness the power of words to express our best, right? Have you ever thought the word "swords" includes "words" in it? As a powerful sword is to a warrior, so are the words to all of us. The sharp words can be as lethal as a sharp sword. Therefore, we must carefully think before we speak. Asking ourselves before we speak: Will my words do more harm than any good? I have seen many self-proclaimed Gurus, and these days on social media, every other person is sharing their thoughts, ideas, experiments, and beliefs. The other evening in one of our outings to a café in south Delhi, my nieces Ishita, and Nikita were excitedly talking about the vlogs, the influencers, and the latest trends while we enjoyed a cup of coffee. I sat on the same table quietly following the conversation to make sense of it, until Ishita turned her face and asked- *"Maasi,* why are you so quiet?" she looked concerned. I replied- "Nope, I am listening to you both and so happy to feel the excitement. Most important, I don't know much about these people you are talking about." I beamed at them. That evening, I ended up getting a list of vlogs to follow from my loving nieces and gathered few of the latest trends to survive in the world. I concluded, Listening is a useful skill, if used correctly.

Although, it made me wonder about the vast influence of social media on all of us. These ideas can be conflicting for a young mind and can misguide novice individuals. Well, it is upon us how we would like to use the social media to spread messages, create content that is meaningful. We have the choice of how we can use our words on social media to raise ourselves, motivate others. There is the power of words that can give hope or diminish it. Words can lead us closer to our goals or totally astray.There is a mention of an interesting practise in the Solomon Islands of the Pacific, wherein the islanders are known to curse a tree to death. They have a special practice of hollering at the tree as they gather around it. They believe the continuous swearing kills the spirit of the tree. As per the claims, it eventually works after several days. Another example of positive words: expecting mothers are encouraged to talk to the baby to help the child learn language, bond with the mother, and develop important skills. Science believes that babies can hear sounds as early as 4.5 months in the womb, and parents' words will have the biggest impact on them.

When it comes to sports, the motivational words from the coach before the match can make the difference in the outcome of the match, be it any sport. In all the above scenarios, words are playing a pivotal role; it is about using the power responsibly. There are numerous ways to express ourselves through words in our everyday lives. We must practice choosing the right way for the scenario at play. One must master the art of communicating concisely. It would be unfair not to mention Haiku when it comes to communicating profoundly with fewer words. Haiku is a Japanese poem writing style that comprises 17 syllables in three lines of 5, 7, and 5 syllables. Haiku answers the when, where, and what. Practicing Haiku can cultivate attention and appreciation of the natural world, language conciseness, and problem-solving. I find it to be a wonderful exercise to practice building conciseness in expressing emotions over time. For example, read a famous poem by a 17th-century Japanese poet, Matsuo Basho:

"An old silent pond.

A frog jumps into the pond.

Splash! Silence again."

It is believed that once Matsuo Basho was walking in a garden with his pupils. The garden had a beautiful pond with red dragonflies hovering all over it. The scene was so mesmerising that one of his pupils expressed a wish to recite a Haiku. His Haiku was:

Red dragonflies!

Take off their wings, and they are pepper pods!

Matsuo Basho wasn't pleased by it and replied to his pupil that what he recited wasn't a Haiku. He elaborated that Haiku isn't about destruction, but it is about the elevation of life, nature, its beauty, and the goodness within it.

He recited the Haiku for the scene:

Red Pepper Pods!

Add wings to them, and they are dragonflies.

A story that wraps the essence of the choice of words and how prevailing the right words can be when combined with concise messaging.

Try these exercises:

- Become conscious of your active listening skills by taking feedback from your peers on – how they would rate your listening skills on a scale of 1 to 5, wherein 5 implies you are an excellent listener.
- Ask questions in your conversation to allow the speaker to encourage the speaker to share their opinions, experiences or ideas with you.
- Listening to podcasts on your topics of interest is a great step in the direction of developing listening skills.
- Expand your vocabulary every week by 5 words to be succinct in day-to-day communications.
- Can you try writing a Haiku when you are out for a walk and someone asks you: "How was your walk?" or when you're back from a holiday in a picturesque town, how would you describe it in a haiku?

Section 4
Lifestyle and Environment

If you have managed to get this far in your reading, you will spend your valuable time going through the next section about simple yet powerful changes to attract good mental health. In the next few chapters, we will focus on bringing clarity not only to our environment but to our minds, too. A clear mind will empower you to step closer to your dreams by allowing you to work unwaveringly towards them. There are times when we can be blinded by our mad rush for success at the cost of our precious relationships and peace of mind. Here is a reminder for you to make yourself a priority. A happy you is a first step towards a happy environment around you.

"Progress is impossible without change, and those who cannot change their minds cannot change anything."

– George Bernard Shaw

Chapter 20
Less Clutter, More Focus

You might have heard of the famous proverb, "Cleanliness is next to godliness." The proverb was first quoted by an English cleric, John Wesley, in the year 1778, and time and time again, it has been used in different shapes and forms.

Moving our direction from west to east, let us talk about the importance of cleanliness in Japanese culture. Japan is a quintessence of cleanliness, which is often related to the values founded by Buddhism and Shintoism. Cleaning and keeping one's surroundings clean is perceived as a form of meditation or a purification mechanism. The streets in Japan are immaculate despite no assigned sweepers or swing bins on the streets. Cleanliness is part of the school curriculum, where children learn from an early age to take responsibility for cleaning what they use. It is natural in Japanese culture to display cleanliness in every nook and corner of the country, be it at home or on the streets.

In matters of Cleanliness, social awareness is at its peak. The office workers and shop staff clean the streets around their workplace, and neighbourhoods hold regular street cleaning events. They have amazed the world with their commitment towards driving the culture of Cleanliness. In 2022, during the Germany-Japan football game, the Japanese team won the match; however, what caught the attention was the Japanese spectators who were seen cleaning up the stadium after the match. They were applauded and left the world in awe, looking for answers for their perseverance to maintain cleanliness.

When I look back at my experience with cleaning in school, it was quite the contrary. When I was in year 8, every day, we were checked during the assembly to ensure our hair was braided, the school uniform was clean, shoes were shining, and there was no nail varnish. I was new to this school, and my previous school didn't enforce braids, so I had a haircut that was unfavorable for braiding. Although my mum tried hard to braid them, they weren't the best braids. As we marched back from the school assembly to our classrooms, the inspecting senior students and teachers caught me for the braids. The punishment was to take a broom and sweep my classroom.

Although I did the assigned task meticulously, it was humiliating for me as that's how I saw it in our society as a child. It took me a few weeks to express my cordiality to escape the task of sweeping. It makes me wonder, had we learned it at an early age in school to take responsibility for cleaning what we use, it would have been a normal chore. After all, it is for our welfare to have clean surroundings.

These Japanese values, practices, methodologies, and rituals are a superb blend of some of the principal lessons of life. As most of us would have experienced these lessons - wonderful; clarity is central; a healthy body fosters a healthy mind, and our mind is the window to perceive the world through our eyes. Cleanliness is required not just for the physical being but for our minds, thought processes, emotions, and memories from experiences. Once we cleanse our minds, we crystallise our feelings to articulate them concisely. The proceeding clarity leads us forward to our goal. In our professional lives, we need clarity on what our roles and responsibilities are, whereas in our personal lives, we need clarity on what the purpose of our life is.

You would have noticed it is frequent to find ourselves distracted, overwhelmed, and unable to organise ourselves. We can pass on the blame to the digital world, endless choices in the online and offline markets for anything and everything. This abstracted behavior often leads to clouded judgment as we are not able to view the dynamics around us clearly. How can we achieve this clarity in this fast-paced environment? Minimise your distractions. The interruptions caused by the buzzing phones, stacks of paper and gadgets on our study table, several decorative items, and everything else that is sitting on your desk. The first step to getting clarity is to adopt cleanliness, right from our personal hygiene to our home and work desks. Start by having only essentials on your desk - a laptop, notebook, power cable, a pen, and a glass of water.

Observe your focus for the next few weeks, and you'll be amazed to see how much you can accomplish in a clean and distraction-free environment. I am sure you have introduced yourself to minimalism, a minimalistic lifestyle. A way of living where intentionality is at the core, and mindless purchasing doesn't exist. You own only what adds value to your life and your loved ones. The non-essential items are removed to create a stress-free environment. By removing these excessive items, you are organising yourself to allocate your limited time, space, and energy only for this finite set of things. Thereby, you develop a calm, clean, and clutter-free environment that leads you to clarity.

Another simple exercise to experience the impact of this little change is to dust the window in your living room, study, or bedroom. What will change? Your view will be clearer, the sun will shine brighter on your face, or you will have a clear view of the outside world. I wish it was that easy-to-get clarity in our thoughts. To be able to do that, it is an inside-out declutter of the thoughts stacked up in our brain space. Scribbling with colors or just making a note of everything that is running in my head and planning what needs my immediate attention relaxes me.

A long walk with my dog aids in my thinking process, and after a long day, a warm shower or a swim prepares me with a clear mind. Use a notebook to declutter your thoughts. Keep it by your bedside to be able to note down any thoughts that crop up in your mind while you are getting ready to sleep. The next morning, take time to go over these notes to plan how you can resolve them. The notebook can be a digital one too; the idea is to save your mind from processing a lot of threads at the same time. When you practice gratitude, seek clarity. One must aim for a healthy body, mind, and soul. As George Bernard Shaw said, "Better keep yourself clean and bright; you are the window through which you must see the world."

Exactly, that's when you are ready to receive the clarity! Imagine you've booked a beautiful cottage for the summer holiday in a picturesque location, and you can't wait to begin your holiday. Months later, when you finally arrive at the cottage, your excited family members open the door and are bedazzled by the immaculate-looking living room and generous preppy bedrooms. Tired after a long drive to your destination, you fall flat on the bed that smells of floral lavender with orange blossom.

You shut your eyes to absorb the scenic views visible from your cottage; calmness surrounds you amidst the playful laughter of your family. Rewind this experience; this time, the cottage you've booked didn't turn out to be as expected. The rooms are unkempt with dirty bedding. Darkness and dampness loom in the house with foul smells emanating from different corners. The expression on your partner's face says it all. Your family is not as excited as you've expected them to be. What was different in the two situations that added calmness to your experience? There can be a number of factors, but one common factor that naturally uplifts your mood is a clean environment.

Various research suggests the importance of a clean, decluttered environment; it fosters clarity of thoughts, improves temperament, and enhances a mental state that is conducive to new ideas. No wonder there is a lot of emphasis on cleanliness right from our early childhood - at home, in school, nursery rhymes, and in fact, I recall our school had a score to rate students on their general hygiene. I recall how I was challenged by my parents to adopt healthy habits for good hygiene and felt equal pressure from the school as they checked our nails, uniforms, and hair during the morning assembly. Not adhering to clean standards had its own consequences of standing out of the class or a round of the grounds in the heat. While at home, I had the duty of dusting the whole house every weekend, and as a reward, I used to get extra pocket money.

As I dusted off the showpieces displayed in the living room, allowing them to look brand new, it gave me a sense of pride and joy. The reward at the end made it more enjoyable. Mom reminded me, "Don't forget to wash your hands after you are done dusting the room!" Cleanliness was integral at home, led by our parents guiding us as young kids to imbibe these values. My mother's cleaning routine over the weekend encouraged me to help her with the chores around the house and accompany her as she dried the fresh-smelling laundry in the sun. I could observe how carefully she arranged the kitchen utensils, wardrobes, and everything in the house spick and span. It was not a secret that she appreciated a well-maintained house, even though it consumed most of her weekend after a busy week teaching at school.

When I look back, it reminds me that being busy or being a working parent is no excuse to let the mess build up in our houses. All we need is discipline, one step at a time, making it a habit to keep things back where they belong. Relook at our wardrobes to give away clothing and bedding that are not in use and create more space. Space for creativity; space for new possibilities. In many countries of the world, there are various charities that take goods in good condition so that they can be repurposed or get a new home. If you prefer to let these items, go to a location for recycling, reuse, and disposal, many waste management companies have facilities where you can drop these items in designated sections for them.

What's the reward for you? I love this question as I love to ask myself each time, I take up a task that I despise. What will I get out of it? Then I imagine walking into a clean house, room, and a healthy mind can be a great reward for me and everyone at home. Another thought that felt rewarding was a surprise visit by a family friend who couldn't stop praising the aesthetics and cleanliness in my home and wanted to know the secret behind it. We all need to find out what that reward could be. Can it be an obstruction-free path to your kid's playroom or an organised wardrobe that saves time for you each morning? The best one for you is a Healthy Mind and a Healthy Body - Mindfulness! A clean room with things in their original places, obstruction-free views, a pleasant fragrance, and saving time to find things through heaps of objects, clothes, books, etc., can contribute to a healthy mind, mood, and body.

Science emphasises the importance of hygiene to maintain a healthy body. Similarly, there have been a number of experiments conducted to understand the impact of a clean environment on the concentration levels of individuals. In fact, I had a similar experience wherein my procrastination led me to a cluttered work desk at home. I was so engrossed in my work that it didn't seem vital to organise papers, notebooks, pens, etc., on my desk. I kept hopping from one call to another, flashing a beautiful background with a sense of pride, while my desk outside the scrutiny of the camera was a mess. Unknowingly, it did add to my mental stress and made it difficult to focus on the point I wanted to drive in these calls, as I scrambled for the piece of paper buried under objects on my desk. A week later, I decided to work from our office.

I felt energised as I worked on my to-do list in our London office. I finished most of the items on the list and felt relaxed too. How did I pull it off? The difference was the environment—a clean environment with limited artefacts on display; minimum distractions supported me in focusing on my tasks. That's when I realised that's the reason why organisations spend millions to build a workplace that delivers an experience for their employees when they work from the office. How do I get this experience every day at home, as I can't travel to London every day? It isn't cheap to travel, even by train, to London, so my home office must deliver the results. The first step was to declutter my study, filled with stationery items. Once I did that, it was time to identify what's required in my room and what's not adding any value to it.

Within a few minutes of cleaning, I could see my focus, which straddled between things, was now consistently catching up with my requirements. It offered me an opportunity to learn and repeat it as a ritual. I started burning incense in the evening to cleanse the energy in my room. You have removed the negative energy that was building around you as you lived with piles of unwanted things stuffed in drawers or hanging from your wardrobe. The clean space allows creativity to flow freely, allows the sunlight to shimmer, and fresh air to breathe.

I want you to take a pause to reflect on what are the things that you've stored or are occupying the space, and you don't need them. Take a look in the garage or storeroom, under-bed storage, your wardrobe, and kitchen and try to connect with what you see around you. Imagine if a few of these things are removed from your storage or room. Does it make any difference to how you feel? Have you used them in the past 3, 6, 9 or 12 months? Start categorising them into piles based on their usage currency. It will show you the collection of objects that you hold but haven't utilised. I did something similar when we were moving homes. That's when we realised that we had collected trivial items like toys, notebooks, showpieces, boxes, books, dog toys, utensils, clothes, and most of them were never taken out of storage.

Nor did once my daughter enquired about these toys that slept peacefully in storage boxes in the cupboard. I had a singular, clearly defined goal to avoid building this undesirable wealth of unwanted objects in my new home. The reason to move into a new house was to acquire more space; I wouldn't waste the space with unwanted objects. Phew, I found a way to strategise using the movers & packers services to transport objects that are valuable and can take up space in our new home. The other strong intention was to build an atmosphere where you will feel at peace rather than feeling flustered with thoughts.

Here is the simple table that I used to support me in initiating a sorting process to ultimately discard the unwanted or donate them to someone who needs it. We can use every 3-6 months for reflection on how we are maintaining our discipline of keeping the cleanliness of our environment, be it work or home. To start, open a notebook and take notes in the below format as you walk around the house, noticing the plethora of things that are waiting to be cleansed, energised, or taken out forever. Don't overwhelm yourself with the whole house immediately; take time to take a tour of your own house, analysing the rooms, looking for objects that can be removed to create more space.

Remind yourself why you are investing time in this activity—to attain a space that reflects you, brings in clarity, and brings a smile to your face. Now start filling this table with details as you pass through the rooms. It is pertinent to call out that it is an iterative process. You might contemplate the potential usability and suitability of these objects, but it will allow you to understand why you bought them in the first place. Naturally, it is a great exercise to encourage healthy spending habits wherein you identify what is important for you. I have filled in the below table as an example for you to use as a reference. Feel free to further add prioritisation in this table to understand which room should be addressed earlier.

Room	What can be removed to create more space?	What can be cleaned to cleanse the energy?	Do I need a replacement?
Living Room	Blue lamp, candle stands, sideboard, DVD collection.	The sofa is outdated and taking more space	Need a compact Sofa, mostly leather fabric-L shaped.
Study Room	Flowerpot, whiteboard, used markers	The curtains and the nest of wires.	Hub to connect wires/ wireless charger and light shade sheer curtains.
Kitchen			
Kids Bedroom			
Wardrobe			

I have tried doing this when we were to move homes. Undoubtedly, I intended to create more space in every room in the new house and get rid of the enormous number of items I had collected over years. As spacious rooms inevitably can capture sunlight and are calming to sit in with the least number of distractions. What about when we spend most of our time at our workplace?

The corporate world has been diligent in focusing on building spaces in offices that allow their employees to focus and flourish. Many enterprise organisations have integrated special work areas within their work environment with a clean, distraction-free environment for employee well-being and to nurture innovation. Clean working environments boost employee mental health as they bring clarity through a better ability to focus. Clarity and cleanliness have something in common, can you guess what? Cleanliness creates an environment for clarity to reside.

Exercise:

1. At this point, use your notebook to reflect before you purchase the new telescope or the latest refrigerator you saw in an advertisement. I would like

to share a top tip that I use when I am out and about and tempted to shop. If I like something, before I buy, I make it a point to ask myself a few questions:

Decision making for	Questions to ask	Answers
Massive Telescope	Do I need the Telescope?	It is a good to have.
	Why do I need it?	To watch the skies with my family.
	Can I live without it for a long time?	Yes
	Where will I store it? Will it need more energy from me than the pleasure it will provide me.	No idea Yes, possibly to store it or set it up in the garden and store it back.

Difficult questions, but worth asking the why, before we start collecting every beautiful and unique item in our homes.

2. Clean Clear Charity (CCC) Method- If you notice your space needs cleansing to allow you to live in a distraction free, calming environment; try this CCC method. Identify the objects that you find distracting. Ask yourselves- Should I clean this, maybe it is dull as it needs a wipe? Should I clear it completely from this space or can someone else make good use of it?

3. We all need motivation to get started with a cleaning spree. Music can be a great companion as you traverse through the heaps of unorganised " stuff" to be sorted. It can help you stay calm during the process and supply you with bursts of energy required. What is great news is that Music can help in developing mental clarity too. Depending on the tracks on your playlist, you can remove the negative emotions affecting your thought process, allowing you to be calmer and think clearly. I enjoy listening to a fast upbeat song on repeat to get the clarity and concentration I desire.

4. Destroying the papers that you don't need or shredding them is a great exercise to clear the clutter from your home and give a signal to your brain that unwanted information can be shredded. Sounds unbelievable? I have tried it numerous times by cleaning the drawers in the study or switching to e-bills where possible. Don't be a hoarder; collect memories.

Cleanliness and Clarity are the two sides of a coin; you cannot have one without the other. A clean environment leads you to think clearly, and a clear mind allows you to organise yourself, including the space you live in. The powers of Cleanliness and Clarity are closely associated to derive synergies and co-exist. We all need both to progress well. However, there can be circumstances wherein health isn't by one's side, irrespective of how clean the environment is, but those scenarios are exceptional or a natural course of our existence. Even then, the cleanliness aspect cannot be disregarded as one needs clarity in thinking to live through it. Cleanliness promotes Clarity! Once you have developed clarity in your thinking, you can sharpen your focus to get to your goal to be healthy or achieve your dreams.

The challenge is, how do we ensure that you get to your goal without getting distracted in this world filled with wonders? Driving your own car is the best advice I received from my driving instructor, and here is my mantra to live by: "Clarity is a wholesome emotion that lusters your inner-view like a brand-new glass and displays you the way forward." Can you see the way forward? Where are you going next? Let's delve into our next chapter to understand the importance of driving.

Chapter 21
Drive Your Own Car and Take Control

"Drive your own car!" - I heard this from my driving instructor when I started learning to drive a car. For years, when I was not in the driver's seat, I played the role of a navigator for my husband. My eyes would be on the road looking for any hazards, reading signboards, and sometimes just looking outside the window. When I started my driving lessons, it took time to switch from the role of a navigator to a driver. I had the steering wheel in my hands, but my habit of scanning the roads continued, resulting in my gaze getting stuck on passers-by, a cute dog, or a child that distracted me. There was this one time wherein I felt that I was lost observing a couple fighting over something on the side of the road I missed the speed limit sign.

Naturally, my driving instructor was attentive; she had caught this habit of mine and warned me a few times before. This time she was loud and clear: "Drive your own car, eyes back on the road." I swerved a bit to the left as I lost my driving position while I looked on the right side of the road. It must have been a short distraction, 1 or 2 seconds; however, it took me dangerously over to the opposite lane. Thank God! What a great reminder to be sure of driving my own car with eyes set on my goal. This sentence went a layer deeper into my soul and prompted me to cogitate how easily we can get distracted and lose sight of our own targets. It is not about ignoring others, but just like any other safety rule, it's a necessity to first drive safely to your desired destination and then you can save the world.

It is important to acknowledge before you drive that the passengers in your car are your responsibility. It is your duty to drop them safely at their destination.

They are partners in your journey who have shown trust in you. Just like we are chasing our ambitions with a higher goal of giving a good life to our family or being able to fund their school or university education. How can we be reckless when we are in the driving seat? We all have our moments when we get to drive, our growing kids are driving their own cars wherein they are responsible for ensuring they are attentive in school, getting the homework done, and learning from their teachers. Having said that, let's not infer that if you witness something untoward while driving, you turn a blind eye to it.

Similarly, even in our personal lives, we support the success of our family members, but we cannot deliver success for them forever. It can be tough as a parent to see our children struggling to take their first flight, but that's how the birds teach their fledglings to fly. The birds must push their young ones from the nest to be able to spread and eventually flap their wings. Likewise, the female tigers feed their cubs until 18–24 months, a time when they can hunt for themselves. There is a famous saying to emphasise the importance of making people independent to allow them to take control of their lives once the right skills and knowledge have been taught. Chinese philosopher Lao Tzu once said, "Give a man a fish, and you feed him for a day. Teach him how to fish, and you feed him for a lifetime."

As we all must learn from different sources before we can apply the knowledge, the learning progresses when we carve our journey. There will be our guides and mentors in our lives guiding us just like the Satnav in our cars, but the steering wheel of your car will be in one hand—that's you! The onus is on you to drive with focus to reach your desired destination and be ready to safely stop and help anyone if your assistance is required. "Most of our miseries stem from others' happiness." I read this behind a truck in India. Impactful, I must say, and those lines stuck with me forever as a reminder when I was setting off on a vicious cycle of comparisons! What do you think?

I am sure many of you drive or have been on the road using different modes of transport. If you don't agree with him, imagine you are driving on a highway, surrounded by several cars, each one going their own way to their destination. You, sitting in your own car, glance over to see those around you, to see vehicles accelerating at different speeds. Despite the urge to ignore these other distractions, a beautiful jet-black Rolls Royce that you've always dreamt of drives past you, leaving you bemused and lost in a whirlpool of thoughts. This car is better than mine, he must be having a more smooth, pleasant journey than me, or perhaps his destination must be grander than anything that I could ever have as my destination!

Was this the experience of the truck driver's life, or did he borrow these lines? Profound words, for sure, yet believe it or not, there have been many moments in our lives when we compare our lives with others and experience despair. Millions of questions hound us day and night: "How did he get the job and not me?", "How come she has two properties?", and soon the desolation turns into anguish and hopelessness. I believe this is the bitter reality of our lives that we need to accept—that we all are unique individuals with a distinctive journey that we pave for ourselves. At no point must we invest our energy in brooding over how our success is different from theirs. Occasionally, we get so trapped in ruminating that we lose control of our own lives. We forget to drive our own car; we take our hands off our steering wheel to watch others as they make way for themselves. We even forget where we intend to go and fall into a dangerous trap of delimiting ourselves as we see our fellow colleague, sibling, friend, or any random individual on social media whizzing through.

The reality is that these thoughts divert you from your own journey and stop you from burgeoning in your own life. These cars are a perfect metaphor for us as individuals driving to their destination, the goal they have been working toward while sculpting their own life. If we cease to focus or believe in ourselves and focus on the lives of others, comparing their lives to ours, we will end up in one long infinite loop of traffic. This example applies in the real world too, wherein you are in control of your direction of travel and focus on your own end goal, the one thing that fuels your passion.

The crucial ingredient for success is to channel our energy to achieve the milestones that we have established for ourselves, congratulate ourselves as we achieve these milestones irrespective of the other cars driving next to us. As you are alien to their purpose or motivation, untold stories, how can you compare? Now, as you continue to drive your car, let me ask a few questions on this scenario:

Do you care about where the other cars are heading to?

Will it impact the journey you are on?

Do you start following these cars, or would you rather focus on driving towards the destination you planned for?

Would you know how far they've travelled?

I don't have to answer these questions nor do you. That's exactly us. Every single day, we have numerous people around us who have a plan and are working to reach their desired destination. Irrespective of their pace and progress, we must continue to pursue our dreams and end goals

When in doubt, just look back to see how far you have traveled and who all are on this journey with you to cheer you. Your proponents or loved ones who are holding the flags of your victory in the race against being a better version of yourself and no one else. Be in control of your emotions; acknowledge them as you continue to drive your own car responsibly.

Here is a list of a few exercises that you can use to shift your focus towards your progress rather than pondering over the green grass on the other side of the fence.

Few exercises for you to explore:

- Make sure to remind yourselves of your short, mid-term and long-term goals. If it is possible for you to have your goals written somewhere you can see them during the day, do that!
- Remember the gratitude journal; spend some time going over the pages you have written in the gratitude journal.
- Try and find opportunities to spend time with your family to get them trained on the essential life skills and teaching good values.

- Have a chat with your colleague or partner to understand your contribution in their lives and how you can help them to be successful.
- Start at an early age for your kids to learn the value of aspiring and chasing dreams.
- A good podcast that talks about the challenges faced by today's successful people can be an adrenaline builder for you to remind you of your goal.

We all must aspire to be a better version of ourselves. It is human tendency to crave what we don't have. Instead of falling into this trap, we must focus on what we can achieve with what we have. What if every single creature starts complaining and comparing about how they look, behave, and what qualities they possess? It will be an endless, fruitless thing to do. We cannot compare our story with anyone's story as we don't know how far they have written it. One thing that we all can do to make life beautiful is to celebrate our differences in our looks, thoughts, statures, and successes. Remember, the sunrises are not the same from all parts of the world; the weather, the culture, the flora, and fauna are all distinct. We have been created to be ourselves, be a better version of ourselves, and shine our light. A mantra to live by is "Drive your own car!"

Section 5
Reflection and Mindfulness

Imagine you are on a long stroll in a beautiful forest with panoramic views of the sky, mountains, and flowing streams. What if your mind is stuck on the project that you must complete and send out to your manager early next week? Are you enjoying the present moment, or are you floating in the thoughts of the uncertain future? Have you found it difficult to keep your mind in control? Did you feel your heart, mind, and body are out of sync as you contemplate between the grandeur of the present moment and the criticality of moments to arrive next week? Here, in the next few pages, let's take a walk together to explore how you can be more mindful to immerse yourself in these timeless moments.

"The present moment is filled with joy and happiness. If you are attentive, you will see it."

– Thich Nhat Hanh

Chapter 22
Heal to Reveal, Meditate to Elevate

The forces of nature are extraordinary; they make us wonder every time we look around us. It was my daughter's birthday, and we got these helium balloons, and she left them to float in the air. I could see these balloons soaring high in the sky, and after a point, we lost sight of them. My daughter wanted to release more balloons in the air, but there were these ordinary balloons that wouldn't rise even after pushing them into the air. The birthday celebration very quickly shifted into a science lesson as she wanted to understand the difference. My husband, Pritam, and I scrambled our brain cells to look for a perfect answer that could satiate her curiosity. Ultimately, we managed to explain to her that the balloons filled with helium can soar, as helium is a gas lighter than the air; the overall weight of the air balloon is less than the air displaced as it floats into the air. It is because of the buoyancy (upward force) that's exerted by the gases. Phew!

Sorted, we have fed a curious mind. Oh no, it made me wonder, isn't it the same for us mortal beings; few can float in the air, and others remain on the ground. The lighter we feel from inside, the higher we will soar. As we grow, we gather so many experiences, prejudices based on our experiences, inhibitions, and create a resistance for ourselves. Our minds are filled with chaos, wanting to achieve multiple goals; however, we are distracted by numerous thoughts or held back due to our experiences or deep-rooted beliefs.

This great concoction inside our minds deprives us of our clarity and ability to lead. Whereas, when we start working on our minds and don't let them astray, we start building a level of focus and concentration. This being the most crucial aspect of controlling our minds. Even in the ancient epic Mahabharata, the greatest warrior of that time, Arjuna, stood in the battlefield to fight for what was rightfully his. He was unable to control his mind. He was filled with self-doubt as his body quivered to see his friends and relatives standing across in an array as enemies. The fear and feeling of compassion overwhelmed his real reason for the battle—the victory of truth over deceit.

Arjun speaks for all of us when he describes the state of his troublesome mind. The mind is restless because it keeps flying in different directions, with different thoughts. It is strong because it overpowers the intellect with its vigorous currents and destroys the faculty of discrimination. The mind is also obstinate because when it catches a harmful thought, it refuses to let go and continues to ruminate over it again and again, even to the dismay of the intellect. Thus, enumerating its unwholesome characteristics, Arjun declares that the mind is even more difficult to control than the wind. It is a powerful analogy, for no one can ever think of controlling the mighty wind in the sky. At this point, Lord Krishna, who is also Arjun's charioteer in the battle, explains to him the importance of controlling the mind by focusing on one's duties and responsibilities without attachment to outcomes, which helps in reducing mental clutter and overthinking.

Think about it, whenever we are invested in an activity, we are under immense pressure to deliver and imagine all possible outcomes. All our fears come alive to inhibit us from even trying to accomplish the activity. What if we know the outcome we desire, but we don't get over-obsessed with the outcome and direct this energy into achieving it with our full might? Have you ever noticed how relaxed one feels after a good swimming session or a long walk? You know that it is good for your health and will make you fit, but you don't think about it every time you swim or worry about it. Consequently, you tend to enjoy it more. It is normal for me to feel so overwhelmed with various conversations I've had during the day, rumbling in my head, analysing what can be done or what I could have done. I can feel the weight of this overthinking. A 45-minute swim has the power to take away my worries, and I emerge lighter from the pool. It has the invisible power of calming our minds and controlling it from running in all directions.

Any of these recreation activities or relaxing spa treatments are great for reducing the levels of cortisol (in our brain); furthermore, research published by Harvard Business Review and other research institutes has emphasised the power of meditation in controlling the restless mind and how it is being adopted by C-suite executives and leaders to be at their very best. What does meditation entail?

Wikipedia describes meditation as – "Meditation is a practice in which an individual uses a technique – such as mindfulness, or focusing the mind on a particular object, thought, or activity – to train attention and awareness, and achieve a mentally clear and emotionally calm and stable state. Meditation is practiced in numerous religious traditions." It is about traveling inside and building an awareness of what's inside us, inside where eyes cannot see, and we need the mind to help us connect.

A common meditative practice is to be aware of our breath. A simple meditative practice of sitting and focusing on our breath releases stress from our body. A Pilot flying an aircraft with around 300 passengers on-board; how crucial it is for a pilot to think with clarity and most important to not to succumb to stress. It is fundamental for them to be in the right state of mind.

No wonder there are various medical tests that they undergo before they can take on the responsibility of flying. How are we different in our personal or professional lives? Be it one or thousands, it is our primary responsibility to care for both our mental and physical well-being. The malevolent forces of stress can drain us emotionally and even deprive us of our basic cognitive abilities. Therefore, in many organisations, there is a focus on supporting their employees and leaders with mental well-being packages that include access to apps that provide guided meditation, Yoga courses, and activities that help to build mental health. We are fortunate that we can work on our skills and rewire them with regular meditational practices. The greatest leaders in history who have been able to control their minds from wandering have exhibited an executive presence throughout the ups and downs of their tenures. If we can gather our scattered energy, it gives us more energy to respond to different situations at work. That's where meditation aids in building focus and clarity.

A decade ago, Harvard conducted research wherein they worked with a group of participants who spent an average of 27 minutes per day practising mindfulness -meditation for around 8 weeks and their responses to a mindfulness questionnaire indicated significant improvements in their overall mindfulness, as it was compared to a pre-research questionnaire. The MR images showed the positive impact of meditation on different parts of the brain- The hippocampus and

Amygdala. The Hippocampus is part of the brain's limbic system and is involved in transferring short-term memory to long-term memory storage, learning abilities and emotional processing of stress and other behaviours.

The Amygdala, part of the brain that controls the "fight or flight" response of our body, was observed to show structural changes to support reduced emotional

anxiety and stress. "It is fascinating to see the brain's plasticity and that, by practising meditation, we can play an active role in changing the brain and can increase our well-being and quality of life," says Britta Hölzel, first author of the paper and a research fellow at MGH and Giessen University in Germany. Interesting how our brain responds to meditative practices. How can we integrate meditation into our daily schedule and make it an integral part of it?

Let me ask you a question: when we say meditation, what is the first image that appears in your mind? Is it an image of a Buddhist monk in a monastery or a Sadhu in saffron clothes, sitting under a tree in deep meditation? You are already on the journey to meditate and elevate yourself if you see yourself meditating instead. The meditation practices need not be cumbersome and can be simple to start with. If you need the motivation to encourage yourself to practice it on a regular basis, try joining a yoga class or practicing using the guided meditation sessions available on various mobile apps.

Here are simple steps that you can take to begin your Meditation Journey:

- Take time to appreciate the nature around you and add it to your schedule to go for short walks or spend time in nature.

- Start your morning without mindlessly scrolling on your phone, and if possible, get a digital alarm clock to prevent you from the temptation of checking your emails
- and social media notifications.
- Calming music in the morning creates an environment to meditate.
- Find a spot where you can sit down with folded legs and closed eyes to focus on your breath as you inhale and exhale; Follow the breath flowing in and out through your body.
- Mantra chanting is another way to develop focus. Remember, with effort and over time, we can be more mindful and bring serenity to our mind. A mind that is not stuck in a flurry of thoughts but a mind that is powerful enough to consider the situation and respond. A mind that is unperturbed by the distractions around you and can focus on its goal to rise. Will you meditate to elevate yourself?

The value of meditation in our daily lives is immeasurable. In our rapid lifestyles, a pause to unwind by connecting with our inner self can be healing. We are running behind our goals mindlessly with a burning desire to attain them at the earliest. What if we could build meditation into our schedules, take time to heal by being in nature's lap? Our potential is limitless; we just need to learn how we can achieve more without the risk of causing burnout. The Dalai Lama says, "All human beings have an innate desire to overcome suffering, to find happiness. Training the mind to think differently, through meditation, is one important way to avoid suffering and be happy." Are you looking for that happiness that brings a smile to your face? Time to read the next chapter to discover the secrets of a mighty smile that illuminates you inside-out.

Chapter 23
Keep Smiling and Let It Shine

A couple of years ago, I was waiting impatiently at the front gate of my residential society, anxiously looking for my taxi to arrive. As I was engrossed in tracking the taxi in the mobile app, a school bus pulled in front of me. Within seconds, my attention shifted to young, excited kids getting off from the bus while they waved goodbyes with much enthusiasm. One young child in particular caught my attention as he screamed-"Mommy!" Running towards a young lady with earphones in her ears; looking into her phone as she walked towards him. Mostly, she was on a call while the kid clutched her hand to walk back towards their home. The expression on the woman's face was blank though for the excited kid, he didn't seem excited anymore. A smile was missing in this whole interaction between the woman and an excited child, happy to be home after a long day at school. Does it matter? Of course, it does.

A simple smile has the power to build stronger bonds, it is an acknowledgement of being heard with a positive mindset. For many, it is a validation to keep going. Finally, my taxi arrived ten minutes late. I swiftly opened the door to take a seat. The taxi driver spoke apologetically- "Sorry mam, there was a lot of traffic, it took me more time to get to you". I smiled at him and said-"It's okay, traffic can be very stressful". I felt so good after choosing a cheerful way to respond to a situation, maybe I was inspired by the contagious smiles of school kids rejoicing a happy day at school. This took me back to my school days; it was so much fun to be back home after school.

I would run into the house to find my mom and embrace her; a smile from her made it worth the wait. Well, the other funny memory is writing letters and before posting them we used to write " Open with a smile, as big as a Nile." on the flap of the envelope. Imagine opening a letter like this in today's times, it will be soothing and calming, for once to think of a smile. Our busy lifestyles, errands to run, timelines to meet, bosses to please, knowledge to compete pushes up away from the essentials of life- A smile to carry you through any river, any sea or a challenge of life. Have you ever tried approaching a challenge with a smile? Naturally, if you have tried, you would be smiling as you will be thinking about your experience.

For me, the challenge was to ride a roller-coaster, a scary roller-coaster at an adventure park. A Team building event was organised in an adventure park, I had no intentions of riding a roller-coaster. Unfortunately, my gaze fell on my group of team members who were queued up for the roller-coaster ride. They were shouting and screaming my name to join them. Trust me, I couldn't say no to them. They were so kind to offer me the first seat on the roller coaster, which is not a great idea for someone like me. I smiled through the process and completed the ride unscathed! I believe the smile instils the energy in me to keep going or do more, in fact to believe in the power of the future.

In one of my professional engagements, there were monthly, quarterly awards, it was a couple of months in the role, but I never received one despite my good work. I was instigated by few to think of reasons why I was missing them. Even then, these award ceremonies never took away my smile; each time someone received an award, I felt a range of positive emotions for their success. The days went by quickly, it was my turn to receive the award, many of them. I smiled back at all who celebrated my success, instigated or tried to instill doubt in me. I was consistent in one thing, I allowed my best self to shine through me, my positivity to keep going shined brightly through me as I worked towards my success, a bright shining story! A simple lesson taught by my mom encouraged me to 'Always choose Smile, if given a choice between Smile and Frown". I heeded her advice to fuel my passion, traverse the hoops of challenges and make my way through the ever-changing landscape of IT and Telecommunications Industry.

Smile is such a strong tool for communication, it connects various cultures, different language speaking people and expresses an individual's openness to participate in a conversation. Few months ago, I was on my way to London from Paris; I queued up for the Eurostar-train. Right in front of me. There was a beautiful baby boy with blue sparkly eyes, a bright green dinosaur soft toy in his hand. He giggled at me, and I smiled back at him each time we had an eye-contact. The next minute after we shared a few giggles, smiles he leapt into my arms, surprising his mom. We connected with positive emotions; a simple smile and it allowed us to be open to more possibilities. Here a possibility to make a new acquaintance was delivered by a simple smile. The Smiles are like sunshine that can reach your soul to let the positive vibes flow through your body. Speaking of Sunshine, last year, it was the harsh winter weather in the month of January. I woke up to wake up Tanishka as she had her swimming lesson in an hour's time. As I opened the window curtains, beautiful sunshine fell on her bed.

"Wake up, Tanu. You'll be late for your Swimming lesson. Good morning love! Wake up!" I tried waking her up for a promising swim in a warm pool in the winter weather.

"Please close my windows, it is too bright" She tucked her face in the duvet as she turned to the other side, away from me".

"Let it shine, my love. We are lucky to see some sunshine today. Let's make the best out of it." I insisted as I kissed her on her forehead.

A thought crossed my mind, we do close the curtains of our minds most of the time. The curtains are drawn so tight that we don't see the light emerging from new knowledge, new experiences, different people, cultures, cuisines and nature. I have known a few people, who believe in ordering the same food in the same restaurant each time they go out for dinner. How will we expand our experiences, if we will not look out for something new? Each day is a new day, it is an opportunity for you, me and all of us to let it shine. The new day is for us to explore, experience and educate ourselves. Every morning, start with a peaceful acquaintance with yourself acknowledging yourself as a being who is fortunate to exist. 99% of the Megafauna are extinct today, we humans are fortunate to survive through nature's play with environment changes, dangerous creatures like dinosaurs, famines, plagues and geological events during the ice age and beyond.

Even if it is a cold winter morning, rub your hands warm to touch your face starting from your eyes, cheeks and the neck and imagine bathing in the sunshine. Let this bring a big smile on your face.

Chapter 24

Look Back and Learn: Embracing Failures

When I look back ten years from now, I believe there is so much that I could have done differently or responded to challenges in a different manner. I have vivid examples of evading problems rather than dealing with them. There was a time in my career wherein I was dealing with emotional turmoil, it made me weak to respond to other curve balls thrown at me. All along, I judged myself on how I responded to a difficult situation. On one of such difficult days, I felt my response was so unprofessional, when I declined to deliver training to a room full of attendees at work because I was going through an emotional low. There was only a limited awareness about the mental health issues back then and a taboo associated with it. In a high-paced competitive environment pausing because of burnout or mental health issues was seen as a sign of weakness. Just saying no on the day of scheduled training, followed by a tough conversation with my manager wasn't all of it. It affected me for long as I found it incredible that someone so professional like me could respond to stress like that.

My inability to accept a low point held me from taking decisions in favour of my career that day. If it was today's Priyanka, she would have stayed calm, would have held her head high while she delivered her responsibilities too. Well, how would I have known this? I had to experience it once to learn ways of responding. No one is perfect to know how to respond to various degrees of challenges. Wisdom joins our path when we start learning from these mistakes in our early lives and career. What did I acquire? I learnt a basic principle of life to look back and learn. Ok, simply looking wouldn't help, one must reflect and incorporate these lessons learnt in our upcoming days of life. Human beings can be stubborn sometimes as we refuse to learn from our experiences. The other evening while I was in the kitchen, Tanishka came all teary eyed to me complaining about Ferro, our dog had snapped at him.

These moments are rare, when I get to explain to her the importance of paying attention to her environment. I am not a cruel mother, just a caring mother who wishes well for her daughter.

"Tanishka, you know he just got his evening-treat, right?" I enquired in awe.

"Yes!" Tanishka replied in a soft voice.

"My love, you know he appreciates space when he is with a treat or guarding it. If you would have engaged him now, he wouldn't have reciprocated well. Did you? Don't you worry, he will be apologetic shortly, don't look at him at all".

"I wanted to play with him" Tanishka added

"Sure dear, you wanted to play but we must read the room. Mr. Ferro is not up for play currently. It is in best interest of all of us to retreat now, to be back later"

Certainly, a simple lesson on managing communication with different personalities will give her pointers for the new relationships that she will build along the way. Our inquisitive, energetic minds can keep us from learning from our experiences, leading us to repeatedly make the same mistakes to get physically or emotionally hurt. What is that the successful people do differently? A lot of things start from understanding how and where to channel their energy. They learn to repeat flawlessly and acknowledge their failures on the road to success.

There are numerous true stories of successful people in various fields who made their way to the mountain of success they aspired for; however, these treks weren't without a fall or a stumble. These stumbles made them further cautious with how they headed to their destination. You know watching these celebrities is like watching a shiny beautiful movie in which they perform at their best.

On my recent trip to Universal Studios in Los Angeles, I got the opportunity to visit behind-the-scenes of popular shows and movies. While our group boarded a tram to ride through Universal, our tour guide explained how the film stars sometimes end up shooting a 2-minute sequence for months to deliver an excellent performance. It made me wonder, how I lose my patience if I must try my hand at something a few times, imagine the mental, and physical strength that would be required by the film stars to complete these sequences. Yes, they do put in an immense amount of energy, but they do end up learning something special from each experience. These learnings become their experience as they progress in their career.

Who doesn't know the mighty Amitabh Bachchan, the legendary Bollywood Film actor? He didn't become a legend by acting only in the first few films; he made his way in the film industry where he rose from numerous flop movies to superhits. Amitabh took a few years to find the right movie role that allowed him to show his very best. When he did find ground underneath his feet, he became a sensation who took over Indian Bollywood with his dominance. "Out of all the bricks that they throw at me, I could build a castle" as Taylor Swift sings it out loud in her song "New Romantics". Amitabh built a castle for himself to climb on to the top by having a growth mindset that allowed him to learn at each step of his career.

Every unsuccessful movie coerced him to understand and work on the reasons for its failure. He didn't give up; he heard his critics to refine his work. Today, he is in the eighth decade of his life and is celebrated across the world for his continued contribution to the film and television industry. Are we any different from Amitabh? We all do the same in our lives like a performer; each day we perform tasks that give us a wide range of experiences to be a better version of ourselves. The only difference is that our performance is not broadcasted or viewed in the cinemas.

We are our biggest audience; we watch our everyday performances to learn from them. Next time you see a beautiful swan swimming effortlessly in a pond, remind yourself she is passing hard underneath the surface of water that appears graceful on the outside. In fact, as a cygnet, she did get some swimming lessons from her parents as she perfected it. Trying isn't hard, failing and acknowledging wholeheartedly that you have failed is an act of courage. What is more courageous is that you don't give up, you course correct to progress.

What if you don't have any experience? Well, you gather experience and when you start, it is an empty sac that keeps filling with your learnings from "University of life". Perfect time to share my latest experience of playing Golf. This summer, while I was in Las Vegas for the Annual Sales Conference, a great time for global teams to connect. People who you see almost every day on your work screens as a tiny square sometimes, but they are across continents. During the Sales conference, we have several gatherings to take the opportunity to know each other more than a tiny square on the screen. To capitalise on the bonding opportunity. Multiple team managers had booked a spot at a 'Top Golf' venue for a lot of us to socialise. Those of you who don't know Top Golf is- It is Golf that is played from a height to hit the ball into the yard consisting of various large circles. You can compete with your team members as your performance gets recorded to be shown on the screen next to you. I highly recommend looking it up on the internet. I had no idea what I was stepping into, compounded by zero efforts to figure out what it is. On the day when we arrived at the 'Top Golf' venue, it was buzzing with lots of people enjoying snacks, drinks, golf and laughter. Time for an honest confession to my teammates, ninety eight percent of my team is experienced males. Wow, an honest confession "I have no idea how to play this thing" I exclaimed.

Brave me, attempted to play it and entertained quite a few people as I seemed to play hockey more than Golf. "I need a trainer, pity please!" I requested help with no hopes of getting it immediately. I ended up securing three fellow-teammates as trainers who taught me in their personal styles- How to hold the club, when to fling it and 'eyes on the ball' as the secret sauce to get it right. At least fifteen attempts until I started enjoying Golf and played it like Golf rather than hockey! At the end of our allocated time slot, I felt a strong urge to keep playing. Let's say parting from Golf was hard for the night.

In this whole scenario, what if I had refused to accept my lack of knowledge, expertise and perseverance to attempt one more time. Thanks to my wonderful team members, I will be starting Golf lessons next month to continue fueling my passion. The whole top Golf experience reminded me of the pearl of wisdom shared by Steve Jobs: "You got to act, and you've got to be willing to fail." - He shared his experience with the world to remind them to ask instead of not trying. Steve called out this ability to ask superior, knowing the answer may be yes or no, there is a probability to fail in the attempt. However, if the answer is yes, you have made progress and no-you know what didn't work. He shared his life experience, how as a 12-year-old kid he found the phone number of Hewlett Packard's CEO to get some free parts for the frequency counters he wished to build.

Not only that, he ended up getting the parts but a job as a summer intern in Hewlett Packard. I know the heading of this chapter says 'Look Back and Learn'- In fact in this book itself there is enough for us to turn back a few pages and reflect. Copy that in your lives to turn around and appreciate where you are standing today. Yes, you stumbled, fell on your face, broke your back, sweated your blood or did nothing at all. Now is your moment to measure up how far you have travelled to get to your destination. Even if you were held back from moving forward to your destination, now is an opportunity to gather your strength, power of wisdom, and passion for your dreams to spring forward.

As we approach the final stretch of our journey together in these pages, I would like you to leave this chapter with a quote by the author of the book "The Rich Dad and Poor Dad"- "Success is a poor teacher. We learn the most about ourselves when we fail, so don't be afraid of failing. Failing is part of the process of success. You cannot have success without failure."

Be brave and set out to seek what the future holds for you, no matter how many times you fall. In the end what will matter is if you continue to seek your future despite these falls and failures!

Chapter 25
Simple Actions: One Day or Day One

Do you recall the feeling of using your pocket money to buy your favourite candy or an ice cream? As a young kid the contentment after having my favourite orange ice-candy was immense; the feeling of getting a treat on a hot summer afternoon was out of this world. Another one from the -"memoirs of childhood" that's close to my heart was the funny screeching beep noise made by a balloon seller as he rode with a bunch of vibrant balloons through the streets announcing his presence. As soon as I would hear him, I would rush to my parents to ask for some money to get an apple shaped colourful balloon with a stretchy string and would celebrate my successful buy on the days, I convinced them to get the money. Another way to be assured of finding my joy was to save money from my pocket money and various chores in and around the house. That's a first step towards understanding how you can work towards your goals by taking simple actions.

Sounds basic, right? Isn't it the basics that connect us to the founding principles of our existence? Just like the primary colours - red, blue, and yellow can create unlimited shades of colour. Similarly, what if we can be as powerful as primary colours, with the ability to blend, without any ego to create disparate colourful experiences. We mustn't doubt ourselves of being capable to achieve our goal. Many a times we wait for 'One Day I will be able to buy it on my own or I will buy it", it begins now and with you. Let today be the 'Day One' of your aspiration. If we start to recognise that we have the power to contribute to create something beautiful, it is achievable. Isn't it same at our workplace, where in we believe in our capabilities, blend in everyone's strength to create something that serves the purpose. These goals may appear to be complex, but we must break the complexity by taking simple actions, every single day.

Moreover, it is not just about simple actions but underlying simplicity that aids in bringing clarity in achieving our goals. Sometimes, too many choices can serve as a distraction in our chosen path or lead us astray. I remember my trips to supermarket for grocery shopping. I would walk in with an intention to buy enough food, snacks and household items to last for a week but would end up buying home décor, clothes, toys for our dog, and my daughter. Financially, it was acceptable and wasn't affecting the balance. However, the amount of stuff I started to hoard at home was unimaginable. Pretty soon, the stuff was moving from the living room to the storage area and finally getting stuffed inside the beds and cupboards. The urge to buy every new and shiny stuff was leading us astray. During Covid, we started ordering food online from the superstore and I started saving myself from the extra stuff and a lot of money. This was the moment I made a small change but lead to a big difference. A simple action to focus on what's needed and not getting distracted changed my life from 'One day' I will sort the stuff I am hoarding to 'Day one' action wherein we inadvertently stopped hoarding. I became conscious of my buying patterns and nowadays, I go with a shopping list in a superstore. Having a clear shopping list prevents me from burning my energy is scanning, observing and developing an urge to buy stuff that's not needed. There are other situations wherein my shopping pattern emerges as a clear weakness. The other day I bought an expensive pair of sports shoes. I took them out of the bag and packed them in the suitcase for an upcoming trip. This revoked the memory of my younger days when I didn't own a first-hand pair of shoes. Being the youngest girl in the family, the shoes from my sisters were passed down to me. My dad promised to buy me a pair of pink shoes if I passed Year 10 with distinction. I did earn a distinction, but he told me once again to wait until I started college. I said to myself "I will own pink shoes one day!", that was my strong desire to own pink shoes.

I saved every single rupee, odd rewards and monetary gifts from aunts to save in a clay money bank with a handmade label "Pink Shoes". That was my reminder to work towards my goal, however silly it sounded. One day, pink shoes were mine after a long wait and I absolutely enjoyed their existence. I could own them because I started on "Day one" to save to get to that "One Day" to own them. I still recall a big bright smile on my dad's face, as he hugged me and said "You did it! I am sorry but I had to let you experience the joy of working towards your goals and enjoying your fruits of labour" he held my brand-new pink shoes in his hands, appreciating them. "Well, I like the Pink Colour, maybe I should get one too" He smiled as he turned on the television for us to watch our favourite game of cricket.

Years went by, I eventually grew independent, buying a pair of shoes wasn't a challenge in fact building a collection of shoes over time. Believe me, many of these pairs were discarded as they were mindlessly bought to be stored. I was utilising lots of space with pairs that never saw the light of the day and spent their lives in the shoe cupboard. More than that, I was confused every time which one to wear; it took a lot of my time and energy in planning. I would literally compare the comfort, looks and colour combination of the shoe before I made up my mind.

Without sounding like a hypocrite, I haven't changed completely and switched to fewer pairs of shoes, clothing or jewellery either. There is a deep-down realisation that I need to work on, but it is not easy due to the fear of society. Contemplation on how I will present myself to them. Will I make myself less desirable, approachable or trustable for progressing in my personal and professional life. Believe me, there are real life people who have embraced simplicity for the greater good. We had a senior Vice president in my tenure with one of the service providers. He had a self-created dress code- White Shirt and Blue pants. I wondered why he would do that? In no time we were exposed to Mark Zuckerberg and many other leaders who believed in maintaining a consistency in what they wore. My personal understanding was that having not to worry about the wardrobe selection every day would save so much time and keep life simple! Isn't it what we want for simplicity? Some of the brands have imbibed the value of a 'KISS'- Keep it short and sweet messaging that appeals to the customer and paved the way to success. "Just Do It" tagline from Nike was behind the huge surge in sales of Nike Shoes and sportswear, when they launched it decades ago.

There was a call for action in the tagline, adverts that motivated people to do more or simply believe wearing Nike they were embracing the message. My mind wandered to think of various other brands how they have captured their target markets with 'Simple' messaging but a message that resonates with their customer base. A powerful messaging is half battle won, if you can connect with your audience. Simplicity can lead to more sales, so why don't we adopt simplicity in our daily lives?

The adverts on the television or while you are at the airport are overwhelming, I was at the London airport's duty-free shopping and the variety of cosmetics, perfumes and brands blew my mind. I had received a long list of cosmetics to be purchased for a friend's sister who was to be married in next few months in India. As I struggled to fulfill the items listed to me, I pondered why do we need so many cosmetics to hide our real looks. Being presentable is one thing but being someone else is another thing. I have seen so many YouTube videos, shorts where various beauty parlours are promoting their skill in transforming the brides. The brides are so very transformed that her own husband wouldn't identify them without the make-up. I am not exaggerating; you must look for bride make-up transformation videos on social media and you will be surprised. Why do we hide ourselves behind layers of cosmetics that are no good to our health, confidence or existence. Ultimately, what matters for a happy marriage? Isn't it a good understanding and appreciation for each other rather than spending lots of money on lavish weddings? Why can't we be striking the balance between being logical and simple? What if the wedding day, could be the 'Day One' of saving money for your first house or a trip to your dream destination?

There has been a surge in many people recognising the need to be our true selves be it our physical appearance or our true emotions. They are adopting a minimalist lifestyle by focusing on less objects and extracting more value out of the existing ones. The business environment isn't any different. There are numerous vendors for a similar technology and numerous technologies by a vendor. The enterprise consumers are being overwhelmed with choice. That's where their investment has been so sporadic and disparate across technologies that adds to their woes of managing relationships, coordination with different vendors.

These enterprises are driving focus to get best out of the existing investment as their growing technology investments are becoming unmanageable with time. Where is Simplicity in all of this and consequently the power?

Our purpose in this world is not to share our opinions on the choices that we make, but rather a strong intent to remind everyone that ultimately, we all are inhabitants of Earth, the same species with different ways of living. Once the level of acceptance rises, our need to hide ourselves behind physical or virtual layers vanishes. Think of the athletes when they run a marathon or a sprint; they do not care about how someone looks, lives, or which country they are a citizen of. They are all champions representing their countries with eyes set on the gold medal. The only things that matter is "Who wins the race?" and "Who believed that one day I will win this gold medal and started from day one to work towards it?" It is simple and powerful.

Quoting Paulo Coelho - "One Day or Day One. You Decide."

It all begins and ends with 'You' exactly as your journey with this book. It is a call for you to pause and reflect on your goals, aspirations that have been in waiting for a perfect time to arrive. Today is the day to take a simple step to work towards them.

Author Bio

Priyanka Shiravadekar is a passionate technologist and seasoned leader with a flair for translating complex ideas into actionable strategies. With over a decade of experience empowering enterprises to make informed technology choices, Priyanka has held pivotal roles at global organisations, leading large-scale transformations and crafting innovative solutions across financial services, IoT, and telecommunications.

Known for her ability to combine an engineer's logic with business acumen, Priyanka thrives on customer engagement and problem-solving. Whether designing architectures for agility, creating white papers, or driving impactful collaborations, she brings a unique perspective rooted in curiosity and continuous learning.

As a believer in the power of personal growth, Priyanka's work is about building bridges between ideas and execution, as well as between people and possibilities. This same ethos inspired her book, *Head, Heart, and Habit: Building a Life You Love*, where she shares her journey, learnings, and reflections. She writes with a heart for connection, inviting readers to pause, reflect, and discover what truly matters.

www.ingramcontent.com/pod-product-compliance
Lightning Source LLC
La Vergne TN
LVHW041220150826
845673LV00001B/461

* 9 7 9 8 8 9 6 3 2 9 6 2 6 *